Converting to Judaism
A Japanese perspective

Kanji Ishizumi

Translator: Kanji Ishizumi
Co-Translator: Kazumi Ikeshima

Grosvenor House
Publishing Limited

All rights reserved
Copyright © Kanji Ishizumi, 2017

The right of Kanji Ishizumi to be identified as the author of this work has been asserted in accordance with Section 78 of the Copyright, Designs and Patents Act 1988

The book cover picture is copyright to Kanji Ishizumi

This book is published by
Grosvenor House Publishing Ltd
Link House
140 The Broadway, Tolworth, Surrey, KT6 7HT
www.grosvenorhousepublishing.co.uk

This book is sold subject to the conditions that it shall not, by way of trade or otherwise, be lent, resold, hired out or otherwise circulated without the author's or publisher's prior consent in any form of binding or cover other than that in which it is published and without a similar condition including this condition being imposed on the subsequent purchaser.

A CIP record for this book
is available from the British Library

ISBN 978-1-78623-777-4

CONTENTS

Forwards	The Lifestyle of a Practising Jew	vii
Prologue	Living in the Present	1
Chapter 1	Fate — *Omnia tempus habent*	3
1.	First Impressions of Judaism	3
	A Foreigner Among Jews	3
	A Highly Successful Minority	4
2.	Major Contribution from a Small Minority	6
	Three out of Ten Nobel Prize Winners are Jewish	6
	Leaders in Education and Business	7
3.	No Open-arms Welcome!	9
	Conversion? You'd be considered to have lost your mind!	9
	By the Book: the Convert's Path	11
4.	Viewing Japan from the Outside	13
	Leaving a High Level Position: my Spiritual Quest	13
	What I Learned in America: How to Think "Outside the Box"	15
	Deciding to Specialise - and Becoming a Legal Maverick	18
	"Let Japan be in Debt": Nationalism vs Globalisation	19

	5.	An Inner Thirst for Religion	23
		A Search for the Meaning of Life	23
		The Comfort of Belonging	24
		New Friends and Acquaintances	27

Chapter 2	Shiur: Getting Closer to G-d through Study	31
1.	Conversion to Judaism: An Academic Pursuit	31
	"Be a Jew Esteemed by Jews"	31
	Reaching out: Religious Trials and Errors	33
2.	An Enquiring Mind vs Blind Belief	35
	"Keep asking questions": Discovering the Joy of Learning	35
	A Lesson from Judaism: How to Live in the Present	37
	The Unfathomable G-d of Judaism	39
3.	An Intriguing Jewish Interpretation	41
	Why G-d has No Name: Judaism and the Great "I AM"	41
	The Hebrew Bible and the Big Bang Theory	43
	The Theory of Evolution and Judaism	45
4.	Profound Insights from the Ten Commandments	47
	What Biblical Scholars Knew: Observing the Ten Commandments is a Tough Call	47
	Honour your Father and Mother: the Importance of our First Relationship	49
	"Thou Shalt Not Steal" Also Applies to Opportunities and Time	51
	"Thou Shalt Not Kill": an Ongoing Debate	52
5.	Rabbi Henry Noach	55
	The Wisest of the Wise but Worldly	55
	A Wealth of Guidance from a Rabbi's Teachings	57
	Respect, but Don't Monopolise your Teacher	58
	The Rabbi and the Japanese Jewish Community	60
6.	Two Thousand Years of Ongoing Education	62
	Internalising the Hebrew Bible	62
	Talmud Education: Finding your own Answers	64

CONTENTS

          Weddings on Wednesdays – a Jewish Perspective:
             The Joy of Discussion and Debate   65
          "Keep Asking Questions": the Jewish Way   67

Chapter 3 Challenges on the Road to Conversion:
          Examinations, Burial, Circumcision....   68

     1. What Makes a Jew a Jew?   68
         Certificate of Conversion: an Identity Card   68
         Three Requisite Examinations   69
         A non-Japanese Burial   70

     2. Circumcision: a Test of Courage   71
         A Surprisingly Major Operation   71
         Post-surgical Pain   73
         Why Circumcise?   75

     3. Challenges, Jewish Courage: Letting
         Discretion be the Better Part of Valour   75
         An Oral Examination   75
         Learning to Cope with the Fear of the
            Terrorist Threat   78

     4. 'Re-birth'   80
         Re-marrying my Wife - at Age 60   80
         Breaking the Wine Glass: Remembering
            Adversity in the Midst of Joy   82
         Public Catechism and Jewish Renaming   84
         The Mikvah: Rebirth as a Jew   86

Chapter 4 Jewish Life – A Simple Life Brings Happiness   88

     1. The Value of Rituals   88
         Rituals and their Meanings: Being a Practising Jew   88
         The Mezuzah: A Spiritual Reminder   91

     2. The Significance of Jewish Family Life   93
         The Emotional and Physical Benefits of a
            Day of Rest   93
         Non-Kosher Foods: Religiously Proscribed   95
         Eating to Live vs Living to Eat   98

3.	Judaism: the Significance of Humour	99
	Overcoming Life's Trials with Laughter	99
	Jewish Wit and Wisdom	100
Chapter 5	How Doubt Gives Rise to Knowledge	102
1.	Nothing in this World is Certain	102
	Shades of Grey vs Black and White	102
2.	Readiness to Accept Others	104
	Netsuke Collection: Shrewd Investment and Risk Management	104
	Going Back to the World as a Jew	
	The Joy of Discussion – "Gold under the Tip of your Tongue"	105
Chapter 6	Making it Work as a Japanese Jewish Lawyer	108
1.	Personal Evolution through Life-long Learning	108
	Intellectual Curiosity and a Thirst for Knowledge	108
	An Intellectual Search for Truth	109
	Maintaining an Open Mind	111
2.	Japan: A Country with Claims to Monoculturalism	112
Epilogue	The Future: a Path of Spiritual Development	114

FOREWORD

The Lifestyle of a Practising Jew

Jews! What thoughts does this word precipitate in your mind?

Some will have a positive image combining industriousness, seriousness, intelligence and creativity. Others may focus on economic achievement. In contrast, there are those who will recall Shylock the miser in the Merchant of Venice and then there may even be some who claim that Jews work to a secret agenda as dark controllers of the world.

Among most Japanese people the domain of the Jew is regarded as a closed book, so here I am going to try to open those pages for you to provide a clearer insight into their world.

I think I am the right person for this task since I am that rare combination, both Japanese and a Jewish convert.

I work as a lawyer, specialising in corporate mergers and acquisitions, business law and worldwide patents. I am also an education consultant, helping Japanese children to study overseas. My own education, post childhood, was at the law schools of both Harvard and Pennsylvania University. The international nature of my work gave me the opportunity to observe Japanese life from the outside whilst at the same time allowing me to interact with many likeminded Jewish people.

The profound intellectual basis of Judaism impressed me to the extent of initiating my conversion. A unique aspect of the religion is the understanding of G-d via the process of questioning. This makes studying religion a ritual activity among Jews. My own decision to embrace this study myself led me to such impressive experiences that I became a convert. By taking you along my path to conversion I hope this book might help you relive many of these experiences with me. In addition, you may be able to make use of them in your future personal life.

As a nation, Japan seems to be flagging and there is widespread concern that it may be going through the process of decay. In the future Japanese people may not always be able to rely on their Government or well-established business institutions.

Historically, Jews had no country on which to rely until the foundation of Israel in 1948. They had always formed an ethnic minority in Christian or Islamic societies and in these circumstances had often suffered discrimination for being different.

However, Jews did not pass out of existence. Instead, they continued to make intellectual contributions to mankind. Of the 7.4 billion people on the planet only 14 million are Jews, yet they account for 30% of Nobel Prize recipients, having made brilliant achievements in science, economics and the arts.

Foreword

The question is: what makes Jews so capable? In spite of all attempts to destroy or subjugate them, their wisdom, intellectuality and stored knowledge could not be destroyed. Jews overcame every imaginable form of discrimination to remain as essential contributors to human society.

I am keen to introduce my fellow countrymen to Jewish life because I can foresee that in future they too may need to find a way to survive in the global community. I am sure they have much to learn from the Jewish example.

I hope you will find inspiration and enjoyment in what you read here and I invite you to experience Jewish life through my personal story.

PROLOGUE

Living in the Present

In my early 50s I suffered a sudden problem with my health and became seriously ill. After state-of-the-art treatment in the US and a change of diet I recovered.

Now I can look back on that experience as beneficial. It taught me about the cost of overwork, the value of life and the true worth of family and friends. It also led me to an interest in mental issues and thence to my conversion to Judaism.

I was treated by Professor Gaynor of the Cornell University Medical School. In common with ancient Japanese thinking he believes that "all illness comes from the mind". He advises his patients to be happy and relaxed and his treatments include the introduction of passages from the sutras of Tibetan Buddhism. He also uses the traditional Indian treatment of Ayurveda to activate the patient's natural curing power. Though I never asked if he was Jewish he quoted passages from the Hebrew Bible and advised me in 2008:

"Kanji, the problems of the present dire economic situation must be keeping you extremely busy. Please do not be concerned about losing anything you have gained since birth because the fear of losing what you have causes the greatest stress to your immune system. Remember the verse in the Bible which tells us 'You were made from dust and to dust you will return.' It is therefore meaningless to allow yourself to be preoccupied by what you have gained in your lifetime. Though it is important to work hard you must avoid fighting things over which you have no power."

Although it might appear easy to ignore circumstances over which one has no power, I found this a difficult process.

Throughout our lives we encounter unforeseen and unpredictable problems in spite of which life continues. Though there are religions which attribute misanthropic reasoning behind such problems Judaism encourages us to learn about G-d to create an ideal society and thence to rejoice and enjoy life as far as humanly possible until the time comes to return to dust.

If you are going through pain please remember the words of Prof. Gaynor and don't stress yourself by trying to hang onto attachments. Perhaps this is one of the secrets of maintaining a happy life.

Remember too that Judaism is also a treasury of collective wisdoms for daily life. I believe they are feasible for everyone to follow and will make for a fruitful life.

CHAPTER 1

Fate – *Omnia tempus habent*

1. First Impressions of Judaism

A Foreigner Among Jews
Perhaps you wonder why I, a Japanese lawyer, the sixth scion of a very conservative merchant house, born in Kyoto, the ancient capital of Japan, became a Jew. I'll tell you the entire story of my journey from the beginning.

I studied at Harvard Law School and the School of Law, University of Pennsylvania, where I made close friends with my fellow students. At Harvard, in 1976 I was admitted to the Institute of East Asian Legal Studies, a department of about 40 students and 10 lecturers.

Many years later, in Washington DC, Jeff, a Harvard contemporary, surprised me while reminiscing over dinner by pointing out that almost all our fellow students and lecturers had been Jewish. Though I was aware that there were Jews in our faculty I had never realised quite to what extent. One cannot identify Jews by the colour of their skin and not every Jew resembles the dark-skinned, hook-nosed stereotype of certain illustrated books, such as those from the Dickensian era. In fact Jews cannot be distinguished from other ethnicities, neither by genes nor blood group.

One of our principal professors at Harvard was Professor Jerome Cohen. I guessed he was Jewish from his surname which, incidentally, means 'a wise man' in Yiddish. However, nowadays surnames are not such indicators of Jewish origin because many Jews changed them to avoid the endemic anti-Semitic discrimination in western countries which continued into the mid-20th century and still exists, though more subtly, today. Especially in the USA, many adopted Anglo-Saxon sounding names.

I had never been bothered about others' ethnicity or origin since I lived in a community of natural American courtesy. Furthermore, I had been too busy with my studies followed by work in the USA, post graduating, to ponder the ethnicity of those I encountered. So, asking Jeff in surprise how he found out that nearly everyone was Jewish, I was rather shocked to hear it was by "instinctive feeling". I suppose, perhaps, his instinct might be similar to that which tells me what part of Japan a person comes from, or which other part of Eastern Asia.

A Highly Successful Minority
Harvard University is one of the most prestigious scholarly institutions in the world and the intense competition makes it extremely difficult for aspiring students to obtain a place. In spite of this, I learned that 30% of its students were Jewish. There are about 6 million Jews in the US, making up less than 2% of the national population. Considering this, the Jewish student-to-university-staff ratio is

remarkably high. Furthermore, all the Jewish students (in both of my law schools) excelled.

The 1970s was a time when Japan attracted global attention for its economic success, a period when high volumes of electrical goods, scientific equipment, photographic merchandise and road vehicles were exported by us to the USA. This created an added interest in Japanese Law in the Institute, where researchers debated in Japanese whilst holding the Book of Japanese Six Major Laws in their hands. The students majored in American Law but minored in Japanese Law.

In the 1980s exports from Japan to the US increased to such a degree that it started to cause major trade friction. To circumvent potential conflict, Japanese companies promoted localisation by setting up manufacturing plants in the US and financial organisations invested to acquire a huge amount of American assets such as real estate, national bonds and equities. As a consequence, the need for Japanese-orientated legal services flooded in to Japanese-speaking solicitors from Harvard and other US law schools so that those Jews who studied Japanese Law enjoyed considerable business opportunities.

In the 1990s, Japan descended into long-term recession following the collapse of its bubble economy. This, in turn, led to the withdrawal of Japanese companies from the US, and divestment of their financial and immovable assets. Once again, legal services were much in demand and those solicitors previously mentioned had yet another money making opportunity. They also switched the direction of their business as Japan showed signs of depression. They studied Chinese, using their knowledge of *kanji* (the pictorial writing system common to both nations) and began offering their legal services to rapidly advancing Chinese businesses. Today, many students and lecturers of East Asian Legal Studies are Jewish, with China their main focus of interest.

My friend pointed out to me that Jewish education, culture and customs produced prescient, studious people who tended to be able to see what was going to happen next while also possessing the flexibility to change their business interests according to the times. This was where my quest for the Jewish way of life started.

2. Major Contribution from a Small Minority

Three out of Ten Nobel Prize Winners are Jewish
My research into Jews revealed that, on the whole, they are a tremendously gifted people.

Of the 7.4 billion people on earth, 14 million, or 0.2%, are Jewish. Slightly fewer than half of these are in Israel, whilst 6 million live in the USA. This tiny minority have contributed significantly to society and humanity, especially in intellectual fields.

An American newspaper survey to ascertain the individuals who had made the greatest impact over the 21st century rated the top three as follows:

1. The economist Karl Marx who, with his book *Das Kapital*, played a significant role in the development of socialism.
2. The psychologist Sigmund Freud, who founded the discipline of psychoanalysis and investigated the depths of human consciousness.

Fate – *Omnia Tempus Habent*

3. The physicist Albert Einstein, who developed his Theory of General Relativity, opening up a new dimension for space studies together with a revolution in physics.

Each of them was born Jewish.

The Nobel Prize is regarded as the best-known and most prestigious award bestowed for cultural or scientific advances in the fields of physics, chemistry, medicine/physiology, literature, economics and world peace. Jews account for approximately 30% of all past recipients. It is noteworthy that 40% of past winners in the field of economics were Jews.

Leaders in Education and Business
I would like to point you towards the many achievements that Jews have made. Not only have Jews produced great thinkers and Nobel Prize recipients, but many of them are also active in the various fields of politics, economics and the arts all over the world.

The second largest population of Jews after Israel is in the USA. Many American Jews choose to enter the professions and large numbers of them have achieved exceptional performances in politics, IT, the media (including cinema), entertainment and music.

For example, the former Chairman of the US Federal Reserve Board Alan Greenspan, the former Chairman of the FRB Arthur Burns, the recipient of the Nobel Peace Prize and former US Secretary of State Henry Kissinger and the former Treasury Secretary of the Clinton Administration Robert Rubin are all Jewish.

In the media, the former owner of The New York Times, the Sulzberger family, is Jewish. The late Katherine

Graham, the president of the Washington Post, was Jewish. The former New York City Mayor Michael Bloomberg, who founded the financial media empire Bloomberg, and the late Joseph Pulitzer, who established the Pulitzer Prize for outstanding achievements in journalism, were also Jewish.

Since its beginnings, there has been a strong Jewish influence in Hollywood, the centre of film production, and several major film companies were founded by Jews. In the music industry, too, a large number of Jews are involved in both production businesses and performing as singers, conductors and instrumentalists.

Jews have also left their mark on the business world: Microsoft's co-head Steve Ballmer, the founder of Intel Andy Grove, the major Wall Street investor George Soros and Leo Melamed, who launched currency futures and derivatives in the Chicago Mercantile Exchange.

Throughout the financial crisis of 2008, two financial groups survived in the US: Goldman Sachs and JP Morgan Chase. The founder of Goldman Sachs was Jewish. Jews have achieved much in Europe as well. The Rothschild family ran a powerful Jewish conglomerate up until the beginning of the 20th century, and the founder of the British investment bank S.G. Warburg & Co. (now part of UBS) was also Jewish.

In 2008, the failure of the Lehman Brothers Investment Bank, founded by the Jewish brothers Lehman in the 1850s, triggered a series of events that affected economies throughout the world to a much greater degree than other failures.

Those facts surprised me, considering that the Jews were a minority yet they have an established presence in the world. Surely, they are not all geniuses or genetically superior? How is it that they produce so many remarkable individuals?

The research increased my curiosity and encouraged me to visit a Synagogue one day in 2003.

3. No Open-arms Welcome!

Conversion? You'd be considered to have lost your mind!

A synagogue is a place of worship, a local Jewish community centre and a Jewish school over which a rabbi, a Jewish religious leader, presides.

The one I visited in New York was also used as a centre where Jewish culture was taught. It was in a modern building on the West Side but, being enclosed by concrete pillars, it resembled a fortress. Visitors were being closely searched for security reasons because of the 9/11 terrorist attacks in the USA. Observing the scene at the entrance, I recognised that Judaism was a closed religion.

"May I have a consultation on conversion to Judaism, please?" I asked at reception. I must say that I had no desire to become a Jew but I thought I would be given an open-arms welcome. Instead, I was treated as a 'weirdo'. "What did you say? A conversion?" said the receptionist with a sceptical look on her face. I couldn't blame her because I, an Asian man, had entered, out of the blue, requesting a conversion. I understood her response better when later I realised that there were very few converts from other faiths even in such a big city as New York.

"The relevant person is not here today. Please come back next Monday. Someone who knows about it will help you then," she said.

However, I only managed to visit the synagogue on a Monday one month later due to my flight back to Japan. This time, there was a man at the reception. I explained that I wanted to have a consultation on the subject of conversion. He explained that I needed to see a rabbi. I asked him, "Is it Mr or Ms Rabbi?" He burst out laughing and said that there were many rabbis. I soon realised that 'rabbi' was a title and broke into a cold sweat with embarrassment. I was so ignorant of Judaism that I had mistaken the title of their spiritual leaders as someone's surname.

He gave me an extension number and told me to phone a rabbi of the synagogue directly to make an appointment.

I was so busy with work at that time that I could only arrange an appointment with the rabbi two months later at her own office in the synagogue. The walls from floor to ceiling were covered with books, and books were piled up high on her desk. It was as if there was a cave made of books in which, in the midst, sat a middle-aged woman. She was the rabbi!

Although she looked gentle, she addressed me rather harshly as follows:

Rabbi: "I heard that you wanted a consultation on a conversion to Judaism. Is this for yourself, Mr Ishizumi?"
Me: "Yes. Should I really say conversion? I am interested in Judaism."
Rabbi: "You'd better not use the word conversion to a rabbi. You would be considered to have lost your mind. Come back to me if you feel like it after reading an introductory book."

Fate – Omnia Tempus Habent

Me: "Then, which book would you recommend, please?"

Rabbi: "Oh, have you neither the motivation nor the time to find one for yourself? This is not the way!"

Having said that, she turned her head back to her computer and got down to her work. Apparently, I had made her angry. I had no alternative but to leave, pretending to be calm while hiding my embarrassment.

I was mystified. Back in those days, I believed that a conversion-seeker was a plus for any religion. Telling them I was a seeker after their faith, I reckoned that I would receive a warm welcome and be asked to make a financial contribution. Some religious groups might operate like this but Judaism was obviously different. They showed no appetite for my conversion.

By the Book: the Convert's Path

Coming away from the rabbi reluctant to acknowledge my foolishness, I was determined to immerse myself in Judaism and someday make her see me in a new light. I popped into the huge bookstore, Barnes & Noble, in the Upper West Side of Manhattan. My face registered shock when I entered the religious book section on the 1st floor. There were hundreds of books on Judaism, Christianity, Islam, etc lined closely together on the shelves. This huge collection of books exuded the great importance of religion in the USA.

A bookstore assistant recommended one of the famous American Complete Idiot's Guide series on *Understanding Judaism*. It was a thick introductory volume of 430 pages, the size of a telephone directory. I also bought an

English pocketbook of the Hebrew Bible which was thicker than a telephone directory at 620 pages.

I started reading them immediately. However, my lack of fundamental knowledge did not allow my brain to absorb their content so instead I decided to start with children's textbooks.

I am linked to a variety of schools through my educational consultancy business. I was recommended an introductory book on Judaism for children by the librarian at a junior high school which responded to my telephone inquiry. I bought it and started reading. The pictures had a nostalgic effect on me as they reminded me of those scenes in *The Ten Commandments* starring Charlton Heston, a film which I had watched when I was at primary school.

After a couple of months of self-study, I visited the female rabbi and told her about my efforts. She listened to me this time saying that she recognised my interest in Judaism. However, she expected me to continue my studies further, pointing out that any talk of conversion should still be a long way off. She recommended that I attend a one-year introductory course on Judaism, twice a week at the centre. Unfortunately, I was not always in New York but travelling all over the world in connection with work.

I asked her if there was a rabbi who could offer private one-to-one tuition. Immediately she took out a thick book from her piles of books, flopped it down on the desk and began flipping through the pages. I later discovered that it was the global directory of about 5000 rabbis. "Oh, here he is," she announced and immediately e-mailed him an introduction to me.

He was Henri Noach, the rabbi of a synagogue, the Japan Jewish Centre, in Tokyo, who guided me on my conversion to the Jewish faith.

4. Viewing Japan from the Outside

Leaving a High Level Position: my Spiritual Quest
I would like to tell you briefly about my background. Looking back, it seems that each event of my life was leading me to Judaism.

I was born in the house of Ishizumi, the Kyoto fan maker/merchants whose business was founded in 1881. The family was originally from Kurotani village in Tanba where, legend has it, fleeing Heike warriors had lived. There, the family first produced Japanese Paper (*washi*) for a living. In the Edo period, one of my ancestors diverted from *washi* production to fan making. (The fans were of the folding type, a Japanese invention, as opposed to *uchiwa*, fixed fans, which are Chinese.)

In all, there were 13 stages in the fan process flow, from ordering to dispatch. These included order intake, fan design, manufacturing management and distribution. From a modern-day perspective this was a production and trading business. In the early Meiji era, exports of traditional arts and crafts were encouraged since Japan had little else to sell. Being appointed by the Meiji Government, my great-great-grandfather and his son introduced Japanese fans at World Expositions as representatives of the Japanese fan industry. They had been chairing the then-Fan Exporters Association of Kyoto. They also travelled from country to country to sell their products.

Back in those days fashionable ladies in Western countries were carrying fans when out and about and at evening parties. Japanese designs gained great popularity with their beauty and elegance. "Ishizumi Fan" grew so big that it dominated all exports from Kyoto and influenced the fans appearing in the paintings of the impressionists Monet and Gauguin. Order forms from British and European royal families can still be seen in my house. King Edward VIII had been one of our customers. We had an enormous 4-metre diameter art fan which my great-grandfather made to exhibit at the Paris Expo. It is now housed in the Japan Gallery of the British Museum. Ishizumi Fan became highly acclaimed as the premier brand throughout Europe.

My great-grandfather's father married a descendant of Sekishu Katagiri, the founder of the Sekishu School of Japanese Tea. I suspect that my grandfather borrowed from the name 'Sekishu' as *seki* and *ishi* are different pronunciations for the same Chinese character, which means 'a small rock'. In fact, my parents' house was the home of the Sekishu School, Kyoto.

The Ishizumis, the direct line of both the Kyoto fan maker and the Sekishu School of Tea, are a long-established, somewhat conservative family. However, my father never restricted my choice of career by demanding that I, an only child, succeed to the family businesses. I think my upbringing had some influence in giving me a diversified perspective on life. Although I was the head of the family, I left Kyoto to become a central government bureaucrat in Tokyo after I had graduated from Kyoto University. In due course, I resigned and became a student at Harvard University. Eventually, I became Jewish. I experienced many intriguing transitions.

Fate – *Omnia Tempus Habent*

I am competitive and also tend to become absorbed in things I like, characteristics which I believe contributed to my good grades at school. However, since my teenage years I had never relished the Japanese style of studying where one had only to regurgitate what had been previously rote memorised for exams.

I matriculated at the Faculty of Law, Kyoto University. I passed the Type I National Civil Service Examination and the bar exam, then entered the Ministry of International Trade and Industry (currently the Ministry of Economy, Trade and Industry). Nowadays, as scrutiny and criticism of society increases, government officials are viewed as somewhat unmotivated. It was very different in 1970, when I entered the Ministry. More was demanded of officials, and their credibility and workplace morale were rising. Many officials felt a sense of responsibility to improve the country and there were many highly-placed senior staff and colleagues to whom I could look up. It was a demanding and challenging occupation, but nevertheless rewarding. I worked there for three years, during which I was promoted to Section Head and produced a new law bill.

I was happy with my bosses, and my work and career were shaping up well. However, I developed a desire to work independently and put myself to the test in an international arena rather than being constrained as a bureaucrat in both lifestyle and career.

What I Learned in America: How to Think "Outside the Box"

I undertook a legal apprenticeship to become a barrister after resigning from the Japanese Ministry of International

Trade and Industry. Back in those days, a working knowledge gained from a two-year legal apprenticeship was required after passing the bar examination in order to qualify as a barrister, judge or prosecutor. Apprentices learned legal procedures such as writing complaints, decrees and preparing indictments. Here, I experienced some confusion.

On the legal training course, an argument was considered won by majority rule whereas those in the minority or with divergent views were bypassed. Professors demanded that we sided with the majority. Indeed, I did not revolt against their majority policies but often felt that these were unreasonable and sometimes strange.

I had been sceptical about Japanese orthodox education ever since I had been a teenage student and wondered about education in the USA. I also wanted to study law at the most prestigious institute in the world to enhance my future business prospects. Considering this, I applied to Harvard where, in 1976 at the age of 29, I was accepted.

I took as many classes as I could for the purpose of completing my course within one year because I was a self-funded student, and consequently I ended up studying more than 16 hours a day, both by attending lectures and putting in many hours in my own time. In the following year my application for a fellowship was accepted and I became a Fellow at the Centre for Study of Financial Institutions in the Law School, University of Pennsylvania. After working for Shearman & Sterling, one of the most prestigious Wall Street law firms, on its Mergers & Acquisitions team, I returned to Japan and established my present law office.

FATE – *OMNIA TEMPUS HABENT*

Education in the USA changed my whole life. My English became fluent and I built up a business network. Moreover, I nurtured the ability to think independently, which now stands me in good stead.

The study of law in Japan taught one to side with the majority and their tests merely required one to rewrite what one had memorised by rote whereas, on the contrary, thinking was encouraged in the USA. They encouraged us to accept that there was usually more than one right answer. Contrary to the Japanese majority principle, they even taught us that there was very often little truth in the majority view. Later, this way of thinking became very useful in my barrister's practice.

Since I greatly appreciated the higher education I had received in the USA, I supported my third child in her desire to study abroad when she was at high school. She might have inherited my spirit of longing for freedom of thought. Through the process of searching and choosing, I found a boarding school which offered teenage boys and girls residential study and an education free from any strictures of government curriculum guidelines.

The school search made me so interested in US education that I qualified as a certified educational consultant of the IECA (Independent Educational Consultants Association) later in 2002. Their objective is to introduce US schooling to aspiring candidates and I act as an intermediary between Japanese students and US or UK establishments. My personal experience of freeing myself from a sense of Japanese stagnation made me want to help those young people who have a desire to launch themselves into the wider world, as I had done.

CONVERTING TO JUDAISM

Deciding to Specialise – and Becoming a Legal Maverick
I was 31 years old when I joined Shearman & Sterling. It is one of the most prominent law firms in the USA and the best on Wall Street, which employs only First Class graduates from prestigious law schools. The firm provides legal services for securities and financial businesses including Citibank. I put in every effort to be taken on but also had considerable luck on my side. Around 1980, Japanese companies were expanding their businesses within America and the firm required a person who was a specialist in both Japanese and US law.

Although I was working excessively hard, as a foreigner it was not easy to assert a strong presence within the firm. It began to occur to me to try to spread my wings in Japan. Besides, I needed to return to Japan to look after my own and my wife's parents even though I had been admitted as a candidate for a Doctor of Law at Harvard Law School. I left the US for Japan and opened the Chiyoda Kokusai law firm at the age of 34, in 1981. There, once again my workload was hectic.

I had served as an attorney for Michael Jackson, who died in 2009. In 1998 he had had the idea of forming a company in Japan to open a theme park and sell Michael Jackson merchandise throughout Asia. He was very shy, quiet and health conscious, subsisting on meagre rations of health food.

Having been overwhelmed by constant criticism of his behaviour in both the western and the Japanese media, sadly Mr Jackson lost all interest in the planned business project. I lament his early death, which happened despite the fact that he was so conscientious about protecting his health.

Possibly due to my Michael Jackson connection and the interest it created, I experienced a sudden increase in business. This included many foreign capital cases which created sensational headlines in the 1980s and 1990s. For example, there was the Texan oil tycoon T. Boone Pickens' attempt to buy out a Toyota subsidiary. Through my work experience in the US my basic position as a barrister was established.

A barrister is obliged to pursue his client's interests, not necessarily acting according to his own principles or opinions but playing the role he has accepted. By throwing himself into a 'role' he thereby becomes merely an actor. I took on a variety of cases under this premise and consequently found myself labelled 'a maverick'.

"Let Japan be in Debt": Nationalism vs Globalisation

Shortly after opening my legal firm, I became an attorney for a gigantic Hong Kong financial conglomerate in its acquisition of a Japanese silk manufacturing company. In pursuing my work I was accused face-to-face, by fellow solicitors and government officials, of being an adulator of "the Hong Kong rat" and of being unpatriotic. The Liberal Democratic Party, then the ruling party, and the government (including the Ministry of International Trade and Industry where I used to work!) worked together to revise a government ordinance to ban foreign acquisitions. As a result, the acquisition I was working on failed.

Twenty years ago I was acting as an attorney for the American oil billionaire T. Boone Pickens in his attempted acquisition of an affiliate of Toyota. On this occasion, my photo and name were exposed to the public by the Japanese media. In consequence, I received the same treatment I had had in the Hong Kong conglomerate's case. I was called every name in the book by the Law Society but also numerous letters and faxes from the public were delivered to my office. Worse still, attempts were made at the highest levels of the government to end my legal career by bringing pressure on businesses to deprive me of any opportunities for work.

I had no alternative but to work out a counterplan: I turned to the US Congress concerning the power of Japan and used my experience of working at a law firm in New York. I lobbied at public hearings and managed to extract verbal evidence critical of Japan from councillors. They exerted an influence on the US Government over the negative balance of trade figures, which at that time featured highly on the agenda at the Japan – US Structural Impediments Initiative. That led the US to demand that Japan liberalise its markets in the 1990s. Finally, the chain of events soothed the emotional response of the protesting Japanese Government.

However, once more, the acquisition plan fell through. The major Japanese automobile makers increased their mutually-held shareholding relationships with suppliers to maintain their competitiveness against companies in the US and elsewhere which they viewed as a threat. However, in the light of subsequent exchange rate developments, this strategy may not have been wise.

After that, I was acting as an attorney to a Chinese tycoon in the case of a hostile takeover of a Japanese-listed rival manufacturer. An American financial conglomerate planned to invest anonymously in the acquisition. The president of a bank and I had numerous discussions and this action was all perfectly legal.

Fate – Omnia Tempus Habent

For a third time, the Japanese parliament and the government reacted against the takeover in the same manner as the previous two attempted takeovers. They created a huge commotion over this issue, claiming that a dubious Chinese tycoon they had never heard of was buying a long-established listed Japanese business. Members of the ruling party put unremitting pressure on us by raising questions in the Diet almost daily, which came close to overwhelming us.

The anonymous sponsor was forced to withdraw from the acquisition, but I will never forget his words: "Kanji, the Japanese care only about themselves. Leave Japanese businesses to their debts." He voiced his frustration with Japan: "I wanted Japan to be one of us, to share ownership and profits after the acquisition. But I don't care any more. The Japanese aren't team players."

His anger stood to reason: The word 'debt' means 'something that is owed or due', but also 'an offence that requires reparation'. 'Equity' means 'the common stock of a corporation' but also 'the state or quality of being fair, impartial, or just'.

Looking back, his words became a reality in 2009. Foreign investors learned to take their money elsewhere and do not even consider Japan for their portfolio allocations.

History repeats itself. Surely, events exactly the same as the ones in the past never repeat themselves exactly, but pent-up feelings and speculations bring about similar events. I have witnessed so many overseas investment projects venturing into Japan and being destroyed, resulting in resentment towards Japan. As long as Japan maintained its economic strength, it attracted world investment, in spite of little effort being made to build cooperative relationships with foreign countries. However, international attention has now shifted to more attractive business partners such as our huge neighbour China and other vast countries such as India, Russia and Brazil.

The Japanese respond with instinctive negativity to anything alien, refusing to accept change and shutting out any apparent non-conformity. They bang down the nail that sticks out and challenges vested interests. I will cite three examples. Takafumi Horie, the founder of Livedoor, and Yoshiaki Murakami, the founder of Murakami Fund and my junior at the Ministry of International Trade and Industry, were each constrained in their business activities by being arrested and prosecuted. Michael Woodford, the former Olympus CEO, failed to gain support from Japanese shareholders in exposing the securities fraud. That was also the result of a Japanese dislike of the 'nail that stuck out'. It did not really surprise me as I had anticipated the outcomes awaiting any mavericks in Japan: the government and the public condemn them.

Foreign elements hold unprecedented power, so I ask you: which is the more expedient – to condemn unprecedented power or to utilise it?

Both the UK in the 19th century and the USA in the 20th century opened their doors to, tolerated and accepted diverse ethnic groups, typically Jews. When members of these groups, typically serving in key posts in the government or public sector, performed to their full potential, they helped establish the countries concerned as world powers.

Foreign influences are appreciated in the UK and the US but crushed in Japan.

Unlike the stereotypical Japanese, Jews in particular take pride in being very different!

5. An Inner Thirst for Religion

A Search for the Meaning of Life

I will go back to talking about my encounter with Judaism in 2003. I had three concerns: 'the meaning of life', 'a realisation of a sense of belonging to a larger community' and 'to stand in a position of equal prominence with the peoples of the world'.

The Hebrew bible says: 'There is a time for everything.' I wouldn't have paid any attention to Judaism if I had encountered it between my 20s and 40s. I was applying myself fully to my career during this time. I was in my late 50s when I became interested in Judaism. My four children had left home. I had secured my position as a solicitor/barrister by dint of hard work but I reduced the very heavy workload of my 30s and 40s due to illness. When my life slowed down, I started soul-searching.

Religion holds no meaning for someone who is not interested but is all important for one who seeks. The fully-fed person does not show the slightest interest in a bread roll but a starved one grabs it. I was experiencing spiritual hunger. Judaism rapidly eased my hunger.

I had had an unsolved question troubling me since my youth and, in those days, it re-emerged as a major preoccupation in my mind: 'What am I living for?'

This is a universal question that almost everyone asks themselves. Time had passed by in a flash while I had been keeping myself too busy studying and working to think about its essence. It was only now I was confronting this question once more.

If I was 'the result of an accident', then my existence itself was meaningless. On the other hand, if my existence was meaningful, then the next questions that begged to be asked were 'Who created me?' and 'What is the meaning of life?' Judaism provided me with answers to these questions. There is a G-d who made us to create a better world. At the same time, Judaism requires us to find G-d's will through seeking. I will examine this in later chapters.

The Comfort of Belonging

Judaism fulfilled my desire to experience life in a way that was beyond my cognisance. It is very hard and lonely to live on one's own. Many people belong to a variety of groups such as companies, leisure groups, professional bodies or communities. I, like them, belong to various groups. However, we realise that we are not necessarily tied to these with a bond of common ethics and beliefs. Perhaps the desire to belong to something greater is buried deep within our minds?

I came to associate myself with Judaism and Jewish ethnicity through my conversion. It is strange to use the word *conversion*. It means to convert oneself from one faith to another faith yet I did not have any before my conversion. I was just the average Japanese with regard to faiths.

Not many Japanese can state their religion when asked. Some scholars argue that Japanese religion is animism although many western scholars do not view animism as a religion. Most Japanese think they do not have any specific religion. Some Japanese were welcomed into Shintoism on their birth, married in a Christian church and will have a Buddhist funeral. The Japanese sometimes pray but to various gods which provide for the syncretism of Shintoism with Buddhism. Many Japanese view religious participation in a negative light due to events such as the toxic gas attack in Tokyo carried out by a fanatical religious group, Aum, which killed many passengers on the Underground.

However, the Japanese view of religion is exceptional in the world. Globally, religion is universal and ultimately the place where people anchor their sense of belonging. Many entrust their spiritual and ethical linchpins there. 'Irreligionists' or 'atheists' are occasionally viewed by some as people lacking in an ethical consciousness.

I am not saying which is right, the Japanese view or that held by the majority of the countries in the world. However, we need to admit that the Japanese outlook is not usual. A person like myself who leads his life by religion sees the Japanese approach to religion as strange.

Now, let me talk about ethnicity.

It is difficult to define the Japanese people. Common denominators may be used to define the race but no determining factors are found.

Is the Japanese language a common denominator? No; because anyone in any country can learn to speak it fluently. Secondly, the identity of the language is not consolidated since languages come through many transitions. Modern and prehistoric Japanese differ in nature, which could possibly mean there was a racial split. Is the nation's land a common denominator? No; the border has passed through many changes. Is the culture of rice cultivation a common denominator? No; it is not uniquely Japanese nor even just found in East Asia. Is religion a common denominator, then? No; that is impossible because Japan has a variety of religions such as Shintoism, Buddhism, Christianity, animism and many others, and even they are often mixed together. In addition, there are many non-religious people in Japan.

The concept of ethnicity is very vague, especially to the Japanese. In spite of that emptiness, it is a key element in deciding matters all around the world. It is just like squeezing pretexts into an empty box and wrapping it up as 'our race'.

In the USA, people are held together according to their ethnicity, such as African, Arabic or Chinese, and develop strong ties within each ethnic group. These ties are so strong that racial conflicts often occur. This isn't just confined to America, it also prevalent in multi-ethnic China and the former Soviet bloc.

Ethnicity does not mean much to people in Japan itself. Some of them might claim that Japan is a country of one single race with its own racial characteristics. I respect their views but I do not agree with them. The racial characteristics of the Japanese seemed ambiguous to me and I felt as if I was a rootless wanderer who did not belong to any particular ethnicity. I was frustrated when I was asked what the Japanese race was.

Jewish converts are granted their status as Jews. Consequently, I gained an inner contentment from the comfort of belonging to something so great.

FATE – *OMNIA TEMPUS HABENT*

The comfort of being Jewish and belonging to Judaism was something I had never experienced. It gave me a feeling of spiritual security and comfort similar to that which we sense when we are with our own mother or close relatives. My conversion to Judaism brought me that.

New Friends and Acquaintances
Judaism fulfilled another of my desires: to align myself with the thinking and religion of people in the world. Here, I will tell you how Japan is seen by the USA, the UK and Europe in an illustrative sense only, drawn from my forty years' experience of travelling back and forth between Japan and other countries in my work.

I was 64 years old in 2012. The expression "Japan is emerging" came into use in my 20s and lasted until my early 30s. Let me explain: A large number of Japanese vehicles were exported to the USA. A book called "Japan as No. 1" was published in 1979. It was the time when Japan began to enjoy increased international recognition.

"Japan Bashing" occurred in my late 30s to 40s. Japan was criticised for earning a trade surplus with the USA. At that time, Japan was at the peak of its bubble economy and was buying up real estate properties in America.

In the late 1990s when I was entering my fifties, it turned to "Ignoring Japan". Japan suffered from the after-effects of its burst bubble economy and was economically depressed. Real estate in the USA and other financial assets were sold and Japan's presence there diminished. As a consequence, the USA diverted its political and economic focus to new emerging economies such as China.

I entered my 60s in 2007. This period could be called "Japan Nothing". China's commercial intention is to dominate the world together with the USA. Japan seems to have entered on a path of permanent decline. It might turn out to be "Japan Vanishing" by the time I enter my 70s.

Would it be an overstatement to say that Japan has never shared values, or for that matter much else, with other countries in any of those periods which I have characterised as of "Something", "Bashing" or "Nothing"? Japan seems to stand outside the world community. Geographically it is located in Asia, but it does not exactly help itself to be heartily welcomed by other Asian countries. Its imperialist past has done little to open the door.

Not only as a country but also as individuals, the Japanese do not throw in their lot with people around the world. It is said that the Japanese are prone to opting out of associating with Westerners, no matter whether they are politicians, bureaucrats or company employees. On the other hand, the Japanese might be seen as outsiders by those who have their own inner space centred around their religions or ethnicity because the Japanese lack any sense of religion or national unity. This is probably the pre-destined path of Japan, which entered a different world culture after the Meiji Restoration (1867-1868).

When Japan opened its shores to Western countries, it resulted in an unpleasant nationalistic reaction to those cultures alongside an unjustified sense of its own superiority. However, and in spite of this, international cooperation emerged. These two elements were the main streams of Japan's modern development and history of thought.

Fate – Omnia Tempus Habent

Occasionally they have overlapped each other or one has been overridden by the other, but those conflicting thoughts have influenced Japan's contemporary history.

Although I can identify with the feelings and emotions present in both, backlash and cooperation, I have opted for a different approach: namely, to become a Jew. This is neither to emphasise strongly the greatness of Japan to the world nor to cosy up to the other people of the world. It is to put oneself on an equal footing and join hands with the world.

Judaism is different from Christianity and Islam yet has some shared features. Although the Hebrew Scriptures make up the Bible of Christianity, they are called the Old Testament. Islam inherited monotheism from Judaism. For this reason, Islam and Judaism have a great deal in common. The prime example is the prohibition on eating pork. The fasting month of Ramadan and the Jewish Festival of Yom Kippur are similar in concept. On becoming a Jew, I spiritually stand on common ground with the believers of Islam and Christianity, two of the world's other major religions.

I meet a variety of people through my work based in the western world. Clearly, these people see me first of all as Japanese, an alien who thinks about nothing but business, one who has different values to them, with neither faith nor a distinct ethnicity, nor a philosophy based on a faith.

When I introduce myself as being a Jew, it is met with surprise and amazement; I am no longer regarded solely as Japanese but as a human with value judgements based on a particular faith. This has happened in New York,

London, Amsterdam, Frankfurt, in fact everywhere. In particular, fellow Jews have accepted me spiritually.

My spiritual thirst made me strive for a faith. As I studied Judaism, my external environment including my social life and personal relationships changed. Being a Jew was the key which opened doors I could not previously unlock in western society.

Once I had an angry American negotiating partner who was a self-proclaimed devout Christian. I replied to his email pointing out his departure from the teachings of the Bible. It was a petty matter but I couldn't help feeling good at making better use of the Bible than the so-called Christian.

When I reflect on my life, the above matters of the soul turned my mind to Judaism.

CHAPTER 2

Shiur: Getting Closer to G-d through Study

1. Conversion to Judaism: An Academic Pursuit

"Be a Jew Esteemed by Jews"
In Spring 2004, I went to see Rabbi Henri Noach in Tokyo. He began our first meeting by saying the following:

Rabbi Noach: There are a variety of religions available to someone seeking a faith – Buddhism, Islam and Christianity, for example. Among them all, Judaism requires the most time and the most laborious study. I recommend, therefore, that you to turn to Buddhism, which is most familiar to the Japanese people.
I: How much time would it require?

Rabbi Noach: It's entirely up to you. If you have a lesson with me for a couple of hours every day, it'd take about two years.

I: That's as hard as a postgraduate course. Unfortunately, once or twice per week would be the maximum I could allocate.

Rabbi Noach: Then, it'd take seven to eight years. Depending on how things go, it might even require more than ten. What about turning to another religion rather than Judaism?

I: (Taking umbrage at his remarks) I never thought it would take so long. It makes me wonder if Judaism is reluctant to accept new followers.

Rabbi Noach: Judaism was founded by the proselyte Abraham, who covenanted with G-d and immersed himself in the new faith. King David and King Solomon were descended from Abraham. Therefore, proselytes draw peoples' attention. As such, they need to study Judaism to the point where they are esteemed by those born into the religion.

I now realised why I was treated in such a reluctant manner. Abraham was the first Jew. He built his faith in G-d through conversations with Him. He went through the procedures that G-d required, then became converted. Judaism discriminated against people like Adam, Eve and Noah of Noah's Ark, who preceded Abraham as Jews.

Shiur: Getting Closer to G-d through Study

Jews have been criticised for their claim of being the chosen people for over 2000 years. Christian societies saw Jews as obnoxious. That contributed to the persecution of and prejudice against Jews. After my conversion, I found this criticism unjust.

G-d appointed Jews as 'the chosen people'. At the same time Jews 'chose G-d'. It was a covenant between Jews and G-d: Jews accepted faith in G-d and adherence to His commandments, and G-d chose Jews for their prosperity. Therefore, Jews believe that they deserve a return for choosing to bow down before G-d. Abraham converted following this bilateral covenant with G-d. Since a convert becomes a Jew by voluntary decision, conversion tests are observed as a matter of course.

I reflected on Rabbi Noach's question. There were two paths in front of me: whether to back down and forget my goal, or to go all the way no matter how long it might take. The only certainty was that I would be wasting my time if I did not commit myself fully to studying. I assumed from the variety of exams and studies I had previously undertaken that I wouldn't have any problems studying Judaism. However, it was actually harder than I had anticipated, though I accomplished it in the end.

Reaching out: Religious Trials and Errors

I was interested in religious experiences when I was a student and visited a monastery and a Tendai Buddhism temple. This was because of my intellectual curiosity, in those days, to find out what religions were. Having passed the age of 50, my more recent quest was a spiritual one.

Previously, I had requested to stay at a Catholic monastery for a few months. There, they had an ordinance for monks, called Lay Brothers, to prepare and serve meals to priests, called Fathers. That did not seem right to me. They had a clear-cut order of precedence whereas G-d, in fact, treats all of us equally. On top of these negative feelings, I was caught smuggling in whisky as a substitute for sleeping pills, so they kicked me out.

Following this, I stayed at a Buddhist temple and spent a few days under the same roof as the monks. The routine was to get up at 4am, listen to a reading of the sutras then have a meal of rice and miso (bean paste) soup only. The High Priest's preaching was very interesting and all the monks were friendly and pleasant.

They explained about the excellence of Buddhahood and the deliverance from earthly bondage. However, those verbal explanations did not convince me because I had never experienced them – and there were no books to read about the road leading to Buddhahood. They also told me that it required years of training and a lifetime of effort, yet even that did not guarantee my reaching the Buddhahood. So I withdrew.

If Japanese Shintoism or denominations of Buddhism was structured, offered accessible introductory texts which could satisfy my intellectual needs and had a curriculum to enable busy people like me to study in different cities in the world, I might have been persuaded. However, if someone wants to study Buddhism in Japan, the only path is to enrol as a full-time student at a Buddhist college for four years. It is even harder to find a school or college which teaches Shintoism in Japan. Even if there was one, its teaching would not be in English. It seems to me that they do not try hard enough to broadcast Shintoism or Buddhism in English to the world.

Shiur: Getting Closer to G-d through Study

When it comes to Judaism, I was advised by Rabbi Noach to peruse the Hebrew Bible, the English translation of which is easily available. He also said that it needed deeper studying. I thought Judaism suited me as it required me to understand each step and to deepen my knowledge rather than undertaking all sorts of hardships or experiencing some of the paranormal phenomena that one might expect from other religions.

2. An Enquiring Mind vs Blind Belief

"Keep asking questions": Discovering the Joy of Learning

Here, I would like to introduce my study of Judaism in detail. I received a private lecture once or twice each week from Rabbi Noach. They were of the highest quality. He gave me copies of his own theses together with those of other rabbis and told me to read them before joining his class. In following sessions his lectures were based on these theses. I studied Hebrew both with him and a Jewish lady once per week.

The course of his lectures continued for three years. All were given as private lessons. Following his lecture on "Who Jews are", he gave me others on Jewish history, the Hebrew Bible, the Torah's 613 Commandments (the Jewish common laws), and the Talmud (the commentary on the Torah).

Rabbi Noach's three years of lectures introduced me to the latest studies and validated the various pieces of evidence within the Hebrew Bible. I found that even a great deal of scientific research did not ensure coherence with the Hebrew Bible. Regarding that, I was advised to continue my reflections until my understanding was complete.

Although it was a long and arduous course I enjoyed it because the Jewish intellectual world was profound and full of surprises, in common with the intrigue of Rabbi Noach's excellent teaching. The more I studied, the greater my thrill: what would I find next?

I will give you an example. An ancient Japanese counting rhyme up to 10 goes 'Hee, Hoo, Mee, Yow, Itsu, Moo, Nana, Yah, Kokonotsu, Toh'. This counting rhyme is also used in old Shinto prayers. In a lesson on Ancient Jewish Society, Rabbi Noach told me that in ancient Hebrew a similar counting mnemonic sounded like 'The G-d of Sun, please appear from your hiding place.'

It reminded me of the Ama no Iwayato of Japanese myths: The world was in darkness since the Goddess of the Sun hid herself in a cave as she was distressed by her brother's violence. Other gods prayed for her to appear.

There could be some connections between ancient Judea and Japan. Some Hebrew characters and Japanese *katakana* characters look alike. For example, 'a' is written 'ア' in *katakana* while Hebrew's 'a' is 'א'. Also, 'e' is written 'エ' in *katakana* while Hebrew's 'e' is 'ה', 'k' is 'ケ' and Hebrew 'ב', 'ך'. Similarly, Japanese 'i' is written 'イ' while Hebrew is 'ל'.

There is a story in Judea of 'the Ten Lost Tribes of Israel'. In the 8th century BC when the Kingdom of Judea was overthrown by Assyria, in the land of present-day Iraq, some tribes were taken away to apparently disappear. It may be nothing more than my fantasy, but one of those tribes could have crossed Central Asia and drifted into Japan. In fact, the German archaeologist Schliemann discovered the ruins of Troy by following the writings of Homer, in his epic poems *The Iliad* and *The Odyssey*.

If children were told the story, they might be intrigued to study history and could thereby make major new discoveries of the links between Japan and Judea.

I am sure you have experiences of intellectual excitement and a sense of anticipation. They are a great source of motivation for study. Such pleasures and enjoyments led me to continue mine. In time, I developed my faith in G-d and experienced a change of perspective.

A Lesson from Judaism: How to Live in the Present

Many religions put an emphasis on the following three selling points: the afterworld, fortune, and faith in G-d. Judaism never discusses them. If my new teachers had kept talking about irrational preternatural phenomena or imposed their faith on me, I would have abandoned my studies in Judaism.

Judaism rarely talks about the afterworld, nor teaches how to get to Heaven. It talks about the "Days of The Messiah", which means that the dead come back to life and perfect peace will arrive. Christianity emphasises this doctrine, which it inherited from Judaism. However, Judaism sees the reality of life. Rabbi Noach taught me that the 13 Principles of Judaism by Maimonides (a great Hebrew scholar in the 12th century), with which all Jews must comply, do not teach us when we might reach these "Days of The Messiah". Judaism does not teach worldly fortunes but gives us 613 disciplines. Principles for our daily life are set out and, though it is hard to adhere to all of them, I do try my best to comply. I will talk about them in detail later. Being a Jew is not intended to be about material wealth. What one gets from it is a sense of inner peace and a healthy life.

I was never told throughout my course of study to simply believe in G-d. The Hebrew Bible talks about a G-d who punishes people harshly. G-d burnt down the depraved cities of Sodom and Gomorrah and killed their people. Jews had been in a state of subjugation. Led by Moses, they escaped from Egypt and wandered around in a desert for forty years on their way to the Promised Land.

The Hebrew Bible says that G-d is harsh on people for their bad behaviour. That is not enough to convince Jews. They have been discussing the reasons for G-d's punishment over thousands of years.

Indeed, a person who accepts G-d on faith attracts disapproval. G-d is the Infinite and Almighty. Jews see it as impossible for men to understand G-d since their intelligence, strengths and life are finite. A creature may never be able to understand his creator. For example, I am the sixth generation of a hand fan maker in Kyoto and do not even know or understand the first generation of my own family, which would take me back to my great-great-great grandfather. Let me introduce another old story.

❋ ❋ ❋

One day, after a flood, a Jew was left up a tree. He was a man of faith. A swimmer came by and shouted to him to hold on to his shoulders. The man refused, saying that G-d would come to rescue him. A boat arrived and the rower gave him a shout to come down from the tree and climb aboard. He again refused, saying that G-d would come to rescue him. The water welled up and he was drowned.

Shiur: Getting Closer to G-d through Study

He went to Heaven and met G-d. He criticised G-d for not coming to rescue him. G-d said, "I sent you rescuers twice, but you did not realise."

❋ ❋ ❋

The story above demonstrates the dangers of blind faith.

The Unfathomable G-d of Judaism

Rabbi Henry Noach says, "The quintessence of Judaism is to question everything. Put simply, never cease questioning." This may help Jews to develop strong rational minds.

I attend services at synagogues and Jewish study groups in many countries such as the USA, the UK, Singapore and Japan. Every rabbi asks us if we have questions. Rabbis themselves question the very words in the Bible. I believe that few leaders of other beliefs instruct their followers to question their religious scriptures.

The Jewish house of worship – the synagogue – is very simple, with none of the fine statues or decorations to be found within many Catholic churches or Buddhist temples. I would say that in this way both Islam and Shintoism are very similar to Judaism. Although G-d has no name, image or being in the Hebrew Bible, He is Almighty. Jews do not represent the image of G-d in any format such as light, colour, shape or fragrance or in any other worldly manifestation. For me, it seems G-d's actions are loaded with contradictions. For example, He loves yet punishes people. Therefore, Jews need to hold a discourse with G-d. Jewish prayer is a conversation with G-d. The Bible is G-d's word. To study the Bible is equivalent to having a lecture from G-d or attending His lecture after reading a textbook. Prayer is to speak to G-d in a similar way that a student asks his professor questions.

I told Rabbi Noach that I did not understand G-d's strangeness. His reply was, "That's right. In the first place, men cannot understand G-d. If someone says he understands G-d, then he is G-d himself – which is impossible." It is interesting. When G-d is beyond our comprehension, studying Him enables us to know only a very slight part of G-d. We are taught that this is only to be expected.

In short, Judaism does not want Jews to abandon their humility when they talk about G-d. Feeling "enlightened", "understanding" G-d or declaring "G-d is this or that" or "I am G-d" leads us into blind faith, which is the antithesis of being Jewish.

What I have said above reflects the characteristics of the Jewish religion. Judaism demands that believers ask for G-d's will. However, this cannot be understood by men. Arguing over one thing or another is typically Jewish.

Some may be prone to view science as the solution to everything or that man has knowledge of virtually everything. Such are arrogant thoughts. Commencing my study of Judaism, I started questioning many matters and found the world was filled with things I did not understand. Many of my previous assumptions broke down in the course of my study of Judaism.

When constantly questioning G-d and thinking of G-d's greatness, I discovered that the divine existence of G-d within me grew bigger daily. A colossal presence beyond men's knowledge must be out there. An enormous presence beyond any stretch of my imagination must be presiding over the world. The study of Judaism differed greatly from my experience of other studies. G-d's activities affect everything in the world. In relation to him, the number of subjects to study is boundless. I was well motivated because my study was directly linked to finding out G-d's will as well as to my spiritual development. Spiritual growth, fulfilment and enjoyment are, after all, the main objectives of study.

3. An Intriguing Jewish Interpretation

Why G-d has No Name: Judaism and the Great "I AM"

At this point, I would like to comment on the style of Rabbi Noach's lectures to me:

Do you know the name of G-d?

Moses was the leader who freed the Jews from slavery. He held a talk with G-d In their dialogue, G-d told him, "I am me" and did not name himself. I will colloquially paraphrase an interesting conversation between Moses and G-d (Exodus Ch.3 from v.13):

Moses: When I go to the Israelites and say to them, "The G-d of your ancestors sent me to you", they will ask me, "What is his name?" So what can I tell them?
G-d: You must tell them: "The one who is called I AM."
Moses: They will ask me, "What is his name?" So what can I tell them?
G-d: I am who I am.
Moses: But suppose the Israelites do not believe me?
G-d: You must tell them: "The one who is called I AM."

As a Jew, Moses was reluctant to accept such unconvincing answers, but G-d overrode him. Regarding the above dialogue, Rabbi Noach and I had the following conversation:

Rabbi Noach: Kanji, What if the Prime Minister of Japan suddenly phones a citizen and says "It's me." What would you do?
I: The recipient would look confused and not know who was calling. The majority of people would be confused. Even if he was the Prime Minister he would need to give his name.
Rabbi Noach: However, if it were G-d, any Jew would recognise Him instantly for His immense presence.
I: What do you mean by that?
Rabbi Noach: If G-d had a name such as 'John' or 'Jane', His presence would be limited. This would be wrong. The G-d of the Jews is one. Therefore, no formality is needed.

That is true. After all, when the phone rings and you take the call, you ask, "Hello, who's calling?" "It's John," the caller replies. People who are distant from you need to identify themselves.

On the contrary, my wife knows who the caller is when I tell her "It's me." Similarly, when my wife calls me, I know who it is. She does not need to identify herself by telling me her name because she is a known and significant presence to me.

Using this telephone analogy, every Jew would know who the caller was when hearing "It's me." This means 'Me' is a known and significant presence among Jews. That is the G-d of Jews.

Amused, I made the following observation: "What a surprisingly logic-chopping religion full of curiously different mindsets!" Rabbi Noach introduced those discussions page by page in the Hebrew Bible. I was drawn into the subject more profoundly each time.

The Hebrew Bible and the Big Bang Theory

I was lectured on cosmophysics when I was studying the Book of Genesis in the Hebrew Bible. Modern science has theories on the Earth's creation 15 billion years ago, of which the Big Bang is one. It is also argued that the solar system in which we live was created 10 billion years after the Big Bang, which means 5 billion years ago.

However, it is written in Genesis in the Hebrew Bible that the creation of the universe took six days. On the first day, G-d commanded, "Let there be light", which was the beginning of the universe. On the fourth day, 'G-d commanded, "Let there be lights in the vault of the sky to divide the day from the night; and let them serve as signs to mark sacred times, and days and years; they will give light on the earth" – and it was so. ' (Genesis Ch1 v14-15) On the fourth day, night and day as well as a cycle of days and years were created. This was the creation of the solar system.

"Let there be light" is suggestive of the Big Bang. If the six days of creation correspond to 15 billion years, one of G-d's days is equivalent to 2.5 billion years. Thus, the fourth day would be 10 billion years later than the Big Bang.

It sounds strange that one day for G-d is 2.5 billion years in modern science, but Rabbi Noach says that could be accurate as the speed of time varies. Einstein's theory of general relativity tells us that the speed of time varies according to the situation at the time. The length of time can be determined by the speed of light. In the Big Bang theory, the speed of light was incredibly fast right after the initial unimaginable explosion. It is calculated to have been some billion times faster than the present speed of light. This being so, one day for G-d could feasibly equal 2.5 billion years for humankind.

After the introductions, Rabbi Noach concluded that there were no discrepancies between the Big Bang Theory and the Hebrew Bible.

I was surprised to have this unexpected lecture on cosmophysics during my study of the Hebrew Bible. Rabbi Noach's lectures spent a fair amount of time on the connection between science and the Hebrew Bible. For example, Jews eat food prepared in the *kosher* style only. I learned wine making, cheese making and bread baking and studied the theory of zymolysis.

Judaism forbids labour or the use of fire during the Sabbath (Friday evening to Saturday sunset). Electricity was discovered in the 19th century. They say that Jews in those days discussed such questions as 'Is electricity fire?' or 'What is burning?' The contemporary conclusion was reached: both fire and electricity comprise the same energy. Therefore, in principle the use of electricity on the Sabbath is prohibited. It was necessary for me to brush up on my knowledge of physics to understand electricity and burning.

Shiur: Getting Closer to G-d through Study

The Theory of Evolution and Judaism

In the 19th century, the British scholar Charles Darwin propounded within the theory of evolution that living creatures evolved in their environment. He declared that men were close to apes. On the other hand, the Hebrew Bible tells us that G-d created all creatures. Which do you think is right?

No matter whether it is a simple amoeba or a complex human being, the design and function of any creature are amazingly elaborate. I am unconvinced by the simplistic account of evolution that life was merely born and formed. It stands to reason that G-d might have stood between the birth of life and the development of form. The theory is called intelligent design and is advocated by many Christian churches.

I have heard that intelligent design is taught at high schools and universities in the southern states of America, where the influence of conservative Christianity is very strong. Legal proceedings are often pursued against the US Government on the grounds that this profane theory of evolution must be banned in schools.

Judaism remains flexible in teaching both approaches. The Jewish counterargument is more profound and more logical than the theory of intelligent design:

Rabbi Noach:	It is not established whether the theory of evolution or the Hebrew Bible is right.
I:	Really? No one can prove G-d's creation?
Rabbi Noach:	No one ever witnessed the point at which an ape evolved into a man. The theory of evolution does not have objective proofs. Neither has any proof. Therefore, we

	cannot conclude that the theory of evolution is right.
I:	Now, why didn't I think of that? I accepted the theory of evolution as scientific but there isn't any scientific proof for it.
Rabbi Noach:	That's right. There are many theories that are believed to be based on science but they are actually our perceived notions. Even if creatures do evolve, I've got to ask you, for what purpose do they evolve?
I:	To adapt to the environment.
Rabbi Noach:	Then, why do they need to adapt to the environment?
I:	To preserve the species.
Rabbi Noach:	There are countless extinct species. Isn't it contradictory to become extinct as the result of evolution?
I:	Hmm…that's true. When evolution ends up as extinction, what is the purpose of evolution?
Rabbi Noach:	When cockroaches, flies and rats have survived over many thousands of years, rare and structurally-complex creatures such as the platypus and dugong are dying out. Why? Is the purpose of evolution to cover the earth with cockroaches? If creatures evolve to adapt themselves to their environments, there should be Japanese penguins for a Japanese climate and Israeli penguins for the Middle East, but there aren't any!

Shiur: Getting Closer to G-d through Study

I:	Hmm…I now don't know why creatures evolve.
Rabbi Noach:	The theory of evolution has an unexplained point.
I:	What is it?
Rabbi Noach:	Basically, organic matter composed of such elements as nitrogen cannot be produced without life-forming activities. In essence, the theory of evolution is saying that living organisms were born from nothing. If we leave this inorganic kettle for 15 billion years, would it become a human being? If we affirm the theory of evolution, it has to happen. Then, is man's earliest ancestor a kettle?
I:	It couldn't be a kettle, could it? Hmm…I am confused.

Rabbi Noach's last counter-question was unique and one that I would have never come up with. I did not manage to respond to him when I was logically challenged in this way. The theory of evolution was only an example of so many untested matters that I had routinely accepted. I previously used to see the theory as real but now I do not know.

4. Profound Insights from the Ten Commandments

What Biblical Scholars Knew: Observing the Ten Commandments is a Tough Call
Do you know the Ten Commandments? Perhaps some of you know them by rote learning. They are Jewish doctrines

given to Moses by G-d, in the Hebrew Bible. Since few people know them all I will briefly introduce them here.

They are, as follows:

1. I am the Lord, your G-d. You shall have no other gods before me.
2. You shall not make for yourself any graven images of anything.
3. You shall not take the name of the Lord your G-d in vain.
4. Remember the Sabbath day, to keep it holy.
5. Honour your father and your mother.
6. You shall not kill.
7. You shall not commit adultery.
8. You shall not steal.
9. You shall not bear false witness against your neighbour.
10. You shall not covet your neighbour's house.

Before I studied Judaism, I once had a conversation with a famous Japanese professor, who criticised both Judaism and the Ten Commandments thus:

'Do not kill' or 'do not commit adultery' are basic commonsense principles. Jews cannot claim that they are anything special. On the contrary, the Japanese code is magnificent. 'Treasure conformity' is written in the Seventeen-Article Constitution produced by Prince Shotoku in the 6th Century.

I realized then that the professor's view was different from mine.

The Ten Commandments are very profound. Rabbi Noach asked me for the reason why the Commandments were listed twice in the Hebrew Bible, in Exodus Ch. 20 and Deuteronomy Ch. 5, where Moses passed on the commandments to the Israelites. The Bible rarely refers twice to a subject.

Rabbi Noach: Why are the Ten Commandments mentioned twice in the Hebrew Bible?
I: Because they are important.
Rabbi Noach: That's wrong.
I: Oh, I thought it was correct.
Rabbi Noach: They are repeated because they are the hardest for men to obey. These are really profound commitments.

I thought, 'That is true. The principle of "You shall not kill" has never been obeyed. In short, the Ten Commandments are rather hard for men to follow though they are very important. Jews have been arguing over them for thousands of years.

Honour your Father and Mother: the Importance of our First Relationship

Having been a solicitor for many years, I have frequently faced many an ugly reality. Too many fiascos elicited by emotion or acts of stupidity have kept me busy. Japan's oft-quoted harmony-orientated ideal for living, to 'treasure conformity', may be admirable but it comes across merely as wishful thinking. If the real world operated through such conformity, every conflict should reach an out-of-court settlement.

I think it is very true that the Ten Commandments emphasise the ethical rules that are basic but hard to obey.

Rabbi Noach talked about one of the Commandments: Honour your father and your mother. The reason given in the Ten Commandments is "so that you may live for a long time in the land the Lord your G-d has given to you" (Exodus Ch.20, v.12). Why does Judaism teach us to respect one's father and mother for life?

Rabbi Noach told with me, "Your parents are the first people in your life on whom you vent your anger and to whom you respond with hatred." We often see a baby in a temper at his mother who has restrained him from what he wanted to do.

"If a child cannot get on well with his parents on whom he vents the content of his frustrations, he is likely to fail in emotional interaction with others. He would have an unfortunate life. What is worse, failure in human relationships would be stressful and impact heavily upon him. That acts counter to the principle of Judaism, which is to be zealous in the realisation of G-d's ideal for us." Therefore, the Rabbi informed me, it emphasises "respect for your father and mother".

An appalling incident happened in Nara in Japan in 2006. A 16-year-old boy came to hate his father who had reproached him for performing poorly in school tests. The boy set fire to his home. As a consequence, his stepmother and her two children were killed. A child whose parents have a broken relationship may lead a tragic life. Judaism emphasises the significance of the relationship between parents and their child for the child itself.

"Thou Shalt Not Steal" Also Applies to Opportunities and Time

"Do not steal" is another discipline from the Ten Commandments. In Judaism, 'stealing' applies not only to property such as money or jewellery, it also includes ideas. It was only 50 years ago that literary works and computer programmes were legally recognised as 'intellectual property', so this too falls under the Commandment.

'Reputation' is another aspect to which the discipline of 'do not steal' applies. Take as an example a bakery of high repute. It is unacceptable to defame it and spread a false rumour that it uses stale flour.

The modern legal question as to how an individual can control his own personal data is a relatively new and important ongoing topic.

It also must be said that mendacious labelling is unacceptable. We must not make a business profit from faked or fabricated goods, technologies or services. The Jewish Talmud prescribes that one should not display fresh and stale vegetables in the same basket. For the past few years, food fraud has been given huge publicity in the Japanese media. However, ancient Jewish morality is far ahead of its Japanese counterpart in certain areas.

Rabbi Noach requested of me that I name further examples of what we should not steal from others. After contemplation, I looked to him for an answer. He suggested there were two more examples that we hadn't discussed.

Firstly, we should not deprive an individual of his opportunities. For example, a man concluded a land deal before another man came and offered a higher price for the same plot of land and took it. Legally, this is called Unfair Competition.

Secondly, we should not steal someone's time from them. Present legal discussions do not incorporate this concept. Some examples are: 'being late for an appointment', 'bargaining with a store owner without any intention to buy' or 'overstaying at someone's house'. The Talmud discusses all these.

Jews respect a man's time. Rabbi Noach became very angry at me once when I was late for my tuition appointment. I came to understand his reason for this. I had acted against the Ten Commandments when I was intending to become a Jew myself.

"Thou Shalt Not Kill": an Ongoing Debate

We had a profound discussion on the 'do not commit murder' injunction of the Ten Commandments. A Jew does not accept this to be 'obvious' without pondering its implications.

Firstly, he questions whether his own self meets the definition of a person. Secondly, he questions whether G-d can kill people. G-d killed other ethnic groups who persecuted the Jews and also unilaterally killed a number of Jews. Jews have discussed these self-contradictions of G-d for thousands of years, yet they have not reached a conclusion which convinces everyone.

A Jew takes his questioning further: "Is it wrong to kill someone in self-defence?", "Is it wrong to execute someone who has killed?" or "Is it wrong to kill myself?" Rabbi Noach spent at least three days on each subject.

In the eyes of the law, the first question is about justifiable defence or emergency escape. The second is about punitive justice or the abolition of the death penalty. The third is about euthanasia and the extent of personal integrity in assisted suicide. They are all weighty issues of modern socio-legal study.

Shiur: Getting Closer to G-d through Study

I will now introduce a view of Judaism about which Rabbi Noach told me. I will write only conclusions without any voluminous reasoning.

For example, Judaism recognises that justifiable defence must stand to reason. Their interpretation of it differs from the Christian view of ultimate love: "Whoever strikes you on your right cheek, turn to him the other also."

Examine the scenario where hundreds of people are thrown overboard from a ship and there is only one plank of wood floating on the sea. Would the first man who grabs the board be justified in shaking off all others to save himself? His deed is an emergency escape that Judaism recognises.

Is the sentence of capital punishment pronounced by the court permitted? Judaism views it as acceptable. Life is of high value, therefore there are some sins only expiable by one's own death.

However, the majority of Jews do not accept euthanasia as it is regarded as similar to suicide. Judaism tolerates neither suicide nor self-harm. According to strict interpretation of the law, orthodox Jews do not use razors in order to avoid harming their skin. As a consequence, they grow beards. Rabbi Noach told me that Judaism did not provide the option to end one's own life in order to ease one's pain. It made sense to me.

I asked Rabbi Noach how 'killing' was identified, and in the same vein what constituted human 'life', since abortion issues are intense in many countries. No precise answer can satisfy everyone regarding what human life is. Catholicism does not permit abortion under any circumstances as the embryo is regarded as possessing human qualities.

The main view of Judaism is that an embryo is not human unless more than half of it has emerged from its mother's body at the time of birth. This does not mean that abortion is permitted. An embryo is a part of the mother's body so abortion is considered as self-harm. However, there are exceptions, such as preserving the life of the mother or a pregnancy resulting from sexual assault.

Euthanasia, a dignified death, justifiable defence, emergency escape, a vegetative state and the definition of death came up for debate about 30 years ago in Japan. The Talmud records that Jews have been discussing these issues for over 2000 years. As a legal expert, I was amazed by this.

As I concluded, deep wisdoms are embedded in the Ten Commandments. Jews build their own inner ethics through discussions on the solid foundation the Commandments provide.

When I turn my focus to Japan, the lack of any establishment of individual inner ethics is a big social issue these days. Brutal crimes, shameless bribery and corruption are evident throughout Japan. In some cases the criminals demonstrate their complete lack of basic ethics when killing people or accepting bribes. Social ethics and morality seem to be disappearing since there is no common ethical foundation for society. We try to educate people but no written principles are available. It seems almost impossible to create such codes nowadays. However, social practices based on the aforementioned were established by the Jews thousands of years ago.

Thus, it can be seen that the Ten Commandments contain deep insights.

5. Rabbi Henry Noach

The Wisest of the Wise but Worldly
I was driven to study Judaism by interesting lectures and the personality of Rabbi Henry Noach. He has been one of my very best teachers. His great teaching skills, personal charm and serious approach to Judaism fuelled my motivation to study.

Jews are wont to select the best person in both character and intelligence to be their rabbi. To be approved as a rabbi is a great honour within the Jewish community. A rabbi is a teacher, a spiritual leader and a community leader. Jews still respect deceased rabbis who are called hakims but do not worship them. They see them as those who had a greater wealth of knowledge than ordinary Jews.

Rabbi Noach was born in Paris in 1952. He attended a primary school in the then-fledgling Jerusalem. His middle school was a Swiss boarding school, where he was badly bullied for being a Jew. These incidents led to his transfer to a high school in New York. From there, he advanced to the University of Brussels in Belgium. After graduating, he studied International Relations at the Hebrew University of Jerusalem, where he earned his master's degree. As his interest in Judaism increased, he next graduated from the Jewish Theological College in Jerusalem and passed the rabbinical examination. He is multilingual, speaking English, French, Hebrew and Japanese. He was a rabbi in Japan from 2002 to 2008.

Rabbi Noach is truly committed to Judaism. I told him once that I read the Bible while taking a bath. He admonished me, stating that Jews must treasure the Bible and G-d. He insisted that I take notes during his lectures since he reasoned that they would make valuable future reading, more especially because books on Judaism were not readily available in Japanese.

He is not only magnificent but also worldly. He became irate when I was late or did not do my homework. He was also meddlesome, even interfering in how I made notes. He nagged me so much that I sullenly objected. Then he hastily sucked up to me like a child. His fairly small build, his skin colour similar to mine, and his dark eyes and black hair gave me a sense of familiarity with him.

As my study progressed, he asked me to add to his knowledge of Japanese. I taught him as a token of my gratitude and realised then that we were both students together. Perhaps being influenced by me, he started taking his outer shoes off in the room.

Rabbi Noach enjoyed a variety of wines when Jews could only drink *kosher* wines that were produced, bottled and opened by Jews. When I remonstrated with him, he reasoned that Jews could enjoy any wines, quoting from books on Judaism in the subsequent lecture and gave me a copy of research papers of deceased rabbis and told me to read them. However, they were simply the quibbles of dedicated recreational drinkers, suggesting to me that Judaism shows a degree of tolerance when it comes to human desires.

I am sure we all have similar experiences of the difficulty of keeping a respectful distance from a teacher. We do expect our teachers to be respectable. However, when they are too dominant we cower in front of them. Rabbi Noach is highly intelligent and respectable, yet at the same time quite a character. These different qualities are balanced within one personality.

A Wealth of Guidance from a Rabbi's Teachings

The world's first compulsory education was introduced by Jews. Around 2000 BC, there was a monotheistic ethnic group in the Mesopotamian civilisation within the Tigris-Euphrates river delta. It is thought that their children were educated at a permanent school.

An ancient Jewish law stated that, for every 150 people, there had to be a teacher. This system guided the next generation and enabled the community to keep producing true experts.

A rabbi was a teacher and a spiritual leader of his community and he often acted as doctor, counsellor and social worker.

Now you can understand why Jews put such a priority on education. Judaism is characterised by the importance it places on study. Jews were consistently persecuted and exposed to loss and privation. They were left with nothing yet they still retained their devotion to learning. Education is reproducible. To produce excellent human resources for the next generation, Jews have consistently appointed the best persons of each generation to be their rabbis.

I meet many rabbis attending synagogues all over the world for Saturday service. All of these rabbis are excellent speakers, listeners and intellectuals. They are so knowledgeable that they can deal with any subject from life counselling in everyday matters to philosophical themes and sophisticated Judaic lectures. They lecture us on Judaism in a manner which creates interest. Rabbi Noach pointed out that all rabbis were capable of making their lectures interesting.

We thrive when we are guided by wise people who offer us advice on every facet of our lives. When I look back on the earlier part of my life in Japan, I find there were very few people who could dispense such wisdom.

Respect, but Don't Monopolise Your Teacher
Although rabbis are excellent leaders and guides, Jews do not monopolise them. Jews typically joke about authority. Rabbis are no exception as fodder for humour and Jews even make fun of them, so here I include a couple of jokes about rabbis:

❀ ❀ ❀

Q. How do religious leaders divide the collection money from their congregations between their religion and themselves?
A. A Catholic priest throws money into a circle drawn on the ground. He says that which lands in the circle is for the church and the money outside it is for himself.

A Protestant minister throws money with his full might towards a line drawn on the ground. He says that the portion which lands over the line is for him and that within the line is for the church.

Q. Then, what about a Jewish rabbi?
A. He throws money up to the sky. G-d in Heaven takes his portion. Whatever comes back down is for him.

❀ ❀ ❀

The joke signifies that the characteristic of Catholics is to depend on G-d, and therefore the Catholic priest accepts what was made for him. In comparison, the Protestant minister works hard for his portion whilst the mean rabbi of Judaism maximises his portion through his understanding of Newton's theories.

❊ ❊ ❊

Joke number 2:
Concerned about his afterlife, a wealthy old man offered 10,000 dollars each to Catholicism, Protestantism and Judaism. However, facing death, he suddenly became worried about money for his afterlife so he asked to be refunded 2,000 dollars from each recipient once he was dead.

When he died, the Catholic priest came and placed 2,000 dollars in his coffin. The Protestant minister did the same.

Finally a Jewish rabbi arrived. He placed a cheque for 6,000 dollars in the coffin and took the 4,000 dollars cash as change.

❊ ❊ ❊

This joke ridicules the secularity of the rabbi and his awareness that the dead cannot cash cheques!

The Rabbi and the Japanese Jewish Community
The main sects of Judaism are: Orthodox, Conservative and Reformed. Unlike governmentally organised Catholic churches or Japanese Buddhist sects, Jewish sects form a less rigid federation. The sects are divided on the differences of interpretation of Jewish ordinances. The Orthodox

adhere closely to all ordinances, the Conservatives follow them in principle and the Reformists respond flexibly to present-day life. Each sect appoints its rabbis. There is no hierarchy of rabbis. Rabbi Noach is a Conservative Jew whose principles I endorse at heart.

Rabbis today are employed by local communities. A synagogue looks for a new rabbi from its own community when an old rabbi leaves. A successful applicant for a post is given a contract. The Japanese Jewish community is strongly influenced by the Conservative tendency whereas the American community is equally split between Reformist and Conservative sects.

There are synagogues in Hiroo, a district of Tokyo, and Kobe. The Jewish community in Japan is small, probably having fewer than 1000 members. The majority of Jews in Japan are employees, and their families, of foreign companies such as American corporations, or Japanese women who married Jews. In addition there are school teachers, and merchants who have established businesses in Kobe or Yokohama.

There are also several diamond merchants within the Japanese Jewish community, concentrated in Okachimachi, Taito ward, Tokyo. They have connections to the diamond businesses in Antwerp in Belgium, Amsterdam in Holland and Jerusalem, the world centres of diamond distribution and trading. Jews have been influential in the diamond industry since it began, finding that diamonds are a highly portable form of currency and therefore a good bet for a successful business.

Osamu Tezuka portrayed the pre-war life of a German Jewish family in Kobe in his historiographic novel, "Adolf". It was about the Japanese ambassador to Lithuania, Chiune Sugihara, who in 1940 saved six thousand Jews under Nazi persecution by issuing transit visas to Japan in spite of the disapproval of the Japanese Government. From Japan, the Jews in the Kansai region helped the refugees emigrate to the USA.

The Jewish community in Japan recruited a new rabbi to succeed Rabbi Noach, who retired in 2008. Any Jewish community faces great controversy whenever they appoint a new rabbi. One who is considered great by some may not always seem so good to others.

The small Jewish community in question was in uproar. Jews are opinionated and extremely assertive, especially when it comes to important religious matters. The community had a stormy discussion and exchanged long emails in English expressing their opinions.

Some people accepted the candidate but others refused and announced that they would depart from the community if he was appointed. Although I was involved in the discussion at first, I withdrew since it interfered with my work.

6. Two Thousand Years of Ongoing Education

Internalising the Hebrew Bible

My study took place via the Jewish educational method called Chavruta, which is almost 2000 years old. It was different from a traditional Japanese school education with its one-sided teaching manner. Chavruta enables learning from discussions between the rabbi and the student. Interestingly, this discussion style was used in philosophical education in ancient Greece. It is used in higher education in the US and the UK. I suggest that this Jewish method becomes a universal principle in education.

Rabbi Noach's lectures were based on the Hebrew Bible and the Talmud, the commentary on the Torah. It is said that the Bible took on its present form about 3,000 years ago and the Talmud about 1,800 years ago. The Hebrew Bible has five main books called the Five Books of Moses. Also known as the Torah, they consist of Genesis, Exodus, Leviticus, Numbers and Deuteronomy. In addition, the Bible contains Prophecy, Nevi'im and Kutuvim. The Hebrew Bible is thus quite voluminous!

The Bible may not be well known in Japan but it is a historic bestseller in other countries, particularly in the West. Why don't you pick one up in a library or a bookstore? It comprises around 1,500 pages in fine print, regardless of its versions. It holds a central position in education and Jewish life.

Jewish tradition says that a child becomes a Jew by being immersed in the Torah. This literally means that the Torah is instilled in a child repeatedly and persistently from when he or she is very small. Jewish parents constantly declare to their children "G-d gave us the Torah" in Hebrew as soon as they are able to talk and listen. They then read the Torah in Hebrew to their children when they become old enough for that. Once children can read they have one session a week throughout the year to cover the 54 parts of the Torah. Children perform this repeatedly until the majority of them learn the Torah by heart.

To my surprise, telling me to cast my eyes over a certain verse, Rabbi Noach quoted it aloud without even seeing it. What's more, he could do that in English and Hebrew. He had an excellent memory and, as he had to read the Bible over and over again, it had been drummed into his head. Jews say that the Bible is to be digested and internalised. Jewish children grow up with the Bible and remain under its influence throughout their lives.

"The Bible is like a fig" is a traditional saying. That is to say that every part of the Hebrew Bible is essential. Figs, unlike other fruits, have no inedible parts. In addition, figs grow slowly but bear fruit throughout the year in the area where the Hebrew Bible is set, while other vegetables and fruits like grapes and dates only ripen at certain seasons. The Bible, especially the Torah, is to be read little by little every day and is to be learned throughout one's life. It continues to bring fruition to the Jew's time on earth.

It is hard to explain the Bible, as you will realise if you attempt to read it. I would name it "The Book of Comprehensive Natural History" for convenience. What I mean is that it is like a museum that displays everything. One of its aspects is as a repository of Jewish laws. It contains many interesting stories somewhat resembling fairy tales and the Psalter is strewn with beautiful words. It has the aspect of a great literary work.

The Bible contains numerous scientific descriptions which include natural phenomena, names of minerals, descriptions of climates and the creation of space. It is also a comprehensive science book filled with science-related subjects. Furthermore, it is a history book of the Jewish people and a book on morals that demonstrates a variety of human relationships. No matter from which aspect we read the Bible, we are given new insights and thoughts. It is both intriguing and fascinating. Access to such knowledge and wisdom helps Jewish children considerably in later life.

In addition, an ethical and moral education based on a common textbook brings a sense of unity to the whole community. Despite the Diaspora, Jews have maintained their unity because of their education, which enables them to hand down this bond to future generations.

Talmud Education: Finding your own Answers
I would like to introduce you to Talmud education.

The Talmud means research and study in ancient Hebrew and is a commentary on the law called the Mishnah. It has 63 volumes in more than 30 books and each book contains about 400 pages. Its wide range of contents comments on daily life such as customs, medicine, health, childcare, dispute resolution, home life and sexual matters. Children start learning the Mishnah at the age of ten and the Talmud when 15 years old.

Here, I will explain the structure of the Talmud. It has the Mishnah at its core and contains various related themes called Gemara, which are accompanied by the thoughts of wise people from the historic past. Any conclusions are left to be drawn by the student.

Reading the Talmud is the basic preparation for study. A student needs to absorb the theory before seeking any further necessary information or literature. A lesson commences with preparation. The teacher encourages his students to debate a theme. Each student maintains his own opinion. Students are allowed to refer to the opinions of wise people from the past but their own original opinions are valued even more. The teacher does not force his opinion on the students but points out where further discussions are required. Other students then present their counter-arguments.

Students spend a whole day discussing one theme. Importantly, discussions do not search for a right answer. The quality of discussion, that is to say questioning and logical consistency, is of prime importance. The following day they do the same on the next theme. It is said that it takes five years to cover all of the Talmud themes. It is central to Jewish life to the extent that the most popular prize in Israel is a complete set of the Talmud.

Weddings on Wednesdays – a Jewish Perspective: The Joy of Discussion and Debate
I will introduce you to one of the themes of the Talmud:

One of the Gemara (themes) is as follows: 'A virgin's wedding must be celebrated on a Wednesday.' Endless discussions on the topic ensue, which might seem nonsense to people on the outside. 'Why on Wednesday?' 'Who confirms the virginity?' 'Is the groom eligible to sue the bride when she is found not to be a virgin?' 'Where and when is the subsequent lawsuit to be lodged?' 'Must they live together until the judgment is given?' 'Must the groom support the bride as part of the divorce settlement? 'How can the issue of virginity be judged if the wedding is held when she has a period?'

To Talmud readers, these day-long discussions play a major part in their education. The important aspect of this education is the pursuit of the answer rather than the answer itself. We are supposed to think freely and extensively in Jewish education. It is typical of Jews to discuss a theme endlessly.

Incidentally, I have come up with a new theory on the theme of why a wedding must be on a Wednesday. According to Jewish customs, the groom is able to dissolve the marriage by bringing the case to a religious court. Family courts were held on Thursday and Monday in Ancient Judea. Judaism is caring in its treatment of women. From these perspectives, I thought more deeply about the theme.

Let's say the non-virginity of a bride has become evident. It is impossible to bring a case to the court on the day following Wednesday when they married as a lawsuit needs to be prepared. Friday and Saturday encompass the Sabbath, when Jews are forbidden from labouring, so they cannot write a complaint. Besides, Friday is the time for an elaborate dinner and Jews are encouraged to have sexual relations on Friday. By this time the bridegroom has most likely cooled off.

However, if their marriage took place on some other day of the week, he would not cool off and would therefore be able to prepare a lawsuit. Thus, for women Wednesday is the best day to get married.

This is my original interpretation and, indeed, I think it is not unfeasible. Rabbi Noach deemed it interesting. I was very pleased about this. I took it as if Jewish thinking had matured in me through my exposure to a 2000-year-old educational tradition. Well, you might disagree and be surprised at the pointlessness of such thoughts.

"Keep Asking Questions": The Jewish Way
Human societies are loaded with contradiction and intricately intertwined with many problems for which there are no easy solutions. As I have already suggested

Shiur: Getting Closer to G-d through Study

from an educational perspective, the process of finding the solution to a problem is often of greater developmental value to the individual than the answer to the problem itself. It is the Jewish tradition to learn through discussion, reason and the social interaction of intellectual argument rather than from the rote memorising of a conclusive answer. Traditionally, Jews learn to question everything from childhood as part of their religious upbringing, even when perusing the Bible with all of its history and wisdom.

CHAPTER 3

Challenges On the Road to Conversion: Examination, Burial, Circumcision....

1. What Makes a Jew a Jew?

Certificate of Conversion: an Identity Card
In this chapter I will write about the path to becoming a convert that few Japanese ever experience.

As mentioned in the opening sentence, Jews are either children born to female Jews or they are converts to Judaism. Such is the make-up of the Jewish people.

Conversion needs the approval of a rabbi. When it is approved, a certificate is issued and the aspiring convert becomes a Jew. Rabbis such as Rabbi Noach, with their deep understanding of Judaism, are given the authority by their council to oversee the process of conversion from heathendom.

Certification of conversion is important to Jews and more especially to recent converts like me. Synagogues are duty-bound to archive the registration of converts; however, many Jews are unable to prove their identity due to repeated depredations during periods of persecution throughout Europe. The majority of converts are women who marry Jews. Male conversions like mine are rare.

What if a Jew converts to Islam or Christianity? Many Jews converted to Christianity due to intolerable oppression in the Middle Ages. They became gentile Jews but could go back to Judaism. Judaism has such flexibility. Once a person is accepted as a Jew, he is regarded thus irrespective of any enforced adoption of another religion.

A child of a Jewish mother can break away from Judaism if he or she chooses. A coming-of-age ceremony called Bar Mitzvah is held at the age of 12 for girls and 13 for boys. By refusing to participate they can break away. The physicist Einstein had received a Jewish education but he refused to be confirmed as a Jew at the age of 13, saying he was not convinced of the existence of G-d. Later he seemed to accept the presence of a G-d regardless of religion.

Three Requisite Examinations

Jews have a right to acquire Israeli nationality. An Israeli passport can be obtained when one proves Jewish identity with a certificate of conversion or a synagogue registration and satisfies certain residential requirements.

In short, Jews around the world can become naturalised citizens of Israel; indeed, I have it in mind to become Israeli too in due course. It should perhaps be noted that 20% of the Israeli population is non-Jewish – the country is also home to Muslims and Christians.

Rabbi Noach asked about my readiness for conversion after I had studied under him for two and a half years. On my replying positively he informed me that I needed to sit a written, an oral and a final exam.

I felt it was very 'Jewish' to set exams for potential converts as it compels them to study.

I tackled the 20 written exam questions at a rate of between one and two per month, producing answers in essay form on a piece of A4 paper. In our following class, Rabbi Noach gave his comments in a discussion lasting almost two hours. The questions were about rules applying to Jewish religious law and prayer together with the content of the Hebrew Bible and Jewish history. Essays were assessed on the level of the discussion they initiated. One question on the nationality law under the Constitution of Israel reminded me of my bar exam.

I found the Rabbi's lessons very useful for the essay exams. I was flattered by my results and even more by the comment that my knowledge on Judaism was above that of most Jews in New York. However, to be then told it was miniscule in comparison to that of most rabbis made me realise I was merely beginning as a student of Judaism.

A non-Japanese Burial

On my conversion, I pledged to Rabbi Noach that I would make arrangements for my body to be buried when I died.

He told me during our studies that Judaism had never accepted cremation. The Hebrew Bible says that "you will become soil again" (Genesis 3 v 9) and on this basis Jews are obliged to commit their bodies to burial.

I asked if it violated the teaching of Judaism to bury cremated bones. Rabbi Noach replied that cremation was not accepted since the Hebrew Bible and Judaism prohibited the damaging of dead bodies in any way.

My father had passed away and, though I spent many years abroad, I still harboured my Japanese wish to be buried with my father and other ancestors in our family grave – though, indeed, burial was otherwise rather rare in Japan. The Rabbi expressed an understanding of my sentiment regarding the family grave but maintained that I would need to reject any idea of conversion if this issue was so important to me.

I did not wish to say that I would give up the study of Judaism, indeed the matter of disposal of my remains would be handled by my four children in any case, so I agreed to take the pledge to be buried.

Though I do not know where I might be when I die, I now completely accept burial, though I realise I will need to make arrangements with my children for my body to be transported to America or Israel for that purpose.

I have positive regard for the Hebrew Bible's statement that "you will become soil again". The thought of becoming skeletonised instantly via cremation does not appeal to me and I consider it better to return to the soil gradually. To be placed under a headstone for eternal sleep as bleached bones does not sound right for me either. Instead, I regard the gradual degrading of my body into productive soil as a peaceful continuance of my life. Thus I progressed along the road to conversion.

Next, I was to encounter another huge issue following on from study and exams. This would be my confrontation with circumcision.

2. Circumcision: a Test of Courage

A Surprisingly Major Operation
Circumcision is the surgical removal of the foreskin from the male genitalia. Rabbi Noach enquired if I was

contemplating the procedure now the written exam was over. He told me it was nothing to worry about, "just a little snip and a little bleeding". However, I felt that the complete removal of the foreskin was going to be a much more serious matter!

In comparison, study was simply a matter of finding the time but this operation was a mind and body experience involving the fear of intense pain. Urination would be difficult for a few weeks and sexual intercourse impossible for nearly two months!

Abraham, the first Jew, had been circumcised for conversion at the age of 99. (I must assume that was the first Jewish circumcision.) Following the operation, he fathered a child, Isaiah, with his wife Sara – quite a feat for a man of his age! Nowadays, boys born to Jewish mothers are circumcised on the eighth day of their lives so they do not remember the pain.

In spite of my forebodings, I made an appointment for the operation with a surgeon approved by the Jewish Community of Japan. In due course I arrived for my operation at a most beautiful hospital. Rabbi Noach came along to witness that it was performed in accordance with Jewish regulations. At first I felt shy about revealing my nakedness in front of him until I realised that, after all I had already undertaken and in consideration of what I was about to endure, my concerns about nudity were trivial.

I signed the surgical consent form, took off my clothes, put on the blue operation gown and entered the pristine operating theatre. I winced at the thought of what I was about to endure.

Next, the nurse arrived and covered my face as I lay on the operating table so I could not observe the impending procedure. Without warning, she commenced shaving my pubic hair and applied an antiseptic smelling like tincture of iodine over the area, including my penis. That completed, she placed a cloth over me with a hole through which my member protruded.

After about 30 minutes the doctor entered the room with Rabbi Noach. The Rabbi stood by my bed and offered a prayer as the doctor proceeded to administer anaesthetic injections. I somehow resisted screaming as he inserted the first needle into my organ. It was excruciatingly painful. A second injection followed, as painful as the first; then a third, a fourth and a fifth, each less painful than the previous, as numbness developed.

Once I was completely numb, I could hear the clink of the surgical instruments as they were taken from the tray. Possibly a knife and a pair of scissors, I thought. I was aware that they were being used to cut the skin but could not see what was going on and felt no pain. I could feel the gauze being pressed against my body and hear each snip. I was aware of bleeding but fortunately the anaesthetic worked perfectly.

At last, the sound of the scissors stopped and I guessed they were wrapping my wound with gauze. The operation was completed and the cover around my face removed.

Post-Surgical Pain

My eyes fell on the Rabbi. He bent over, kissed my cheek and hugged me firmly, confirming that the operation had been completed according to the Jewish requirement. He looked so pleased and showered me with praise for the covenant with God he had just witnessed and for the commitment I had made in my determination to achieve my faith-related goal. I was deeply moved.

Next, the surgeon brought me the severed skin and asked if I wanted to keep it. How could I possibly discard a part of my body that had been with me for 60 years? So now it resides in a container in my fridge at home: a piece of skin three or four centimetres wide and fifteen centimetres long. I have written IMPORTANT on the container to ensure that nobody in my family mistakes it for a piece of bacon!

The surgeon left the theatre, possibly for the next operation, while the nurse offered me painkillers for the post-anaesthetic pain. In spite of bravely boasting that I could endure the pain in order to be re-born as a Jew, I accepted the pills – just in case!

Two or three hours later and back in my home, I got myself into a predicament. As the anaesthetic wore off I was overwhelmed by excruciating pain and became terrified to go to the toilet. Though I now readily resorted to the painkillers, the agony continued unabated for three days while I tried to attend to pressing work in my office. I didn't dare reveal myself to the other men in the toilet so had to lock myself in the cubicle when I needed to relieve myself. I felt like an inverted version of the Invisible Man where the only thing others could see of me was my bandaged penis!

At last, on the fourth day, the pain began to subside, though I continued to bleed so much that the blood saturated my underwear and soaked through to my trousers. I resolved the problem with incontinence pads which bulked out my trousers embarrassingly until, at last, on day 7, the bleeding stopped. Eventually, I was able

Challenges On the Road to Conversion

to remove the bandage to see the gauze and stitches for the first time. These gradually fell off as I showered.

So that was it! I was circumcised! Lighter in body – and in pocket to the tune of 150,000 yen (about £1,000 at the time of writing).

Why Circumcise?
So, why is circumcision practised in the Jewish Religion?

The Hebrew Bible says: "Every man child among you shall be circumcised." (Genesis C17 V10) The Bible also states that "it shall be a token of the covenant between me and you" (Genesis C17 v10), that is to say a reminder of the contract I have made with God.

However, as Jews we do not follow the orders of the Bible without logic. Rabbis have long analysed the reasoning behind circumcision. As well as it being a statement of one's covenant with God, they believe it teaches us the importance of sexual self-control. They also consider that circumcision has many health benefits for men and their partners with whom they have sexual contact. The circumcised penis is less likely to carry infections such as Aids or other often seriously dangerous sexually transmittable diseases. Some people also argue that, once one is circumcised, it is easier to control sexual desire.

From my personal perspective, my circumcised penis is my own constant reminder of my religious commitment, each and every day.

3. Testing for Jewish Courage: Letting Discretion be the Better Part of Valour

An Oral Examination
Around the time that my wound had completely healed I was given an oral examination by the elders at a synagogue

in Hiroo, Tokyo, on a Sunday (not a day of rest in the Jewish religion). I was called into a room where I found Rabbi Noach and two elders, my examiners, sitting behind a table. I recognised the elders as heads of foreign companies in Japan but had been unaware of their faith.

I was shown to a seat opposite them and immediately plied with questions. It was reminiscent of my stressful oral bar examinations forty years previously.

The interview ran as follows:

Elder 1: I hear you are a busy lawyer. Shabbat (the Jewish day of rest) commences Friday evening, which means you cannot perform any work until Saturday evening. Can you commit to it?
I: I will.
Elder 2: Will you be able to come to the synagogue to pray on Shabbat, Friday evening?
I: I will observe Shabbat, the most important commandment.
Elder 2: You must not even make a phone-call on Shabbat. You should refrain from driving too. Would you be tempted to drive?
I: I will avoid driving and take the Tube and bus instead. However, when in the West Coast of America I will need to drive to reach a synagogue.
Elder 1: Will you wear the kippa (the male headware) daily? For that matter, will you be allowed to wear the kippa in Japanese courts?
I: Yes. I will wear it and I assume that judges will not object to such a tiny covering on my head.

Challenges On the Road to Conversion

Elder 1: Will you be able to keep the dietary commandments? Octopus, squid and shellfish are forbidden.
I: I have already switched my diet to fruit and vegetables for health reasons.
Elder 2: You are often in China on business, where pork is an integral part of the diet. How do you plan to avoid it?
I: Yes, avoiding pork in China is not easy, especially since the Chinese use lard for cooking vegetables. However, I will only use restaurants which serve steamed vegetables, and where these don't exist in the smaller towns I will consume only fruit.
Elder 1: Will you fix a Mezuzah on the doors of your home and office? Are you aware that it is necessary?
I: Yes, I will.
Elder 2: Will you be able to pray three times per day?
I: Yes I will, although there may be occasions where it is not possible. However, I will at least attend the synagogue every Saturday morning.
Elder 2: I have heard that you cannot read Hebrew yet. What are you doing about it?
I: I have already been having tuition and will study hard so as to be able to read the Torah in Hebrew.

I will explain about the Jewish Custom aspect of the above interview later. Up to this point I had been nervous but managed to answer smoothly as I had studied and prepared. However, the next stage was the tough one:

Elder 1: Even now, Jews are subjected to the risk of persecution or discrimination. Do you still wish to become a Jew?

"Here it comes, as anticipated", I thought. I had considered this matter as I walked through the street to the exam venue though had failed to find the answer.

I replied, intentionally missing the mark, "I spend a great deal of time in both the US and the UK, in New York, Los Angeles and London, and haven't encountered prejudice to date, so I guess I'll be OK." I knew this was not what the elder wanted. As expected, he became more specific:

Elder 2: That's not what we asked. I'll put it more clearly. You could be killed if an antagonistic Nazi-style regime takes power. You could be exposed to terrorist ordeals, for instance if the plane you are on is hijacked by anti-Jewish terrorists and they start by threatening to kill Jews. Under such circumstances would you raise your hand in admission of your faith?

This was the hardest question over the four years of study under the Rabbi. The result of the whole exam depended on my answer to this question.

Learning to Cope with the Fear of a Terrorist Threat
The question was not about a 'what if' situation. Against the backdrop of the political climate in the Middle East, Jews could come under terrorist attack. Many American Jews, immigrants from Eastern Europe, lost their relatives to Nazi brutality.

In the 21st century we may feel, though, that not so many Jews have experienced persecution. Let me tell you about an Ethiopian rabbi who, when in Japan in 2008, recounted his own experience. Everyone hung onto his words so attentively that we forgot to eat our meal – so unusual for Jews, who love eating and table discussions.

There are many black African Jews in Ethiopia. The Ethiopian military government had been rounding up and imprisoning them since the end of the 1980s and, though they were not executed, they were deprived of food and starved to death.

The rabbi was one of the first to be captured, though he managed to escape while the guards were distracted. He hid in a farm shed that day and set off towards the border under cover of darkness, hiding each subsequent day and walking only through the night-time. Once well away from camp he took the risk of changing this pattern and boarded a bus to hasten his way to safety.

Terrifyingly, not far along the road the bus was stopped at a military check-point, where two soldiers boarded, waving their machine guns at the passengers. They ordered everyone on board to hold their passports or alternative IDs above their heads.

The rabbi, who was without any identification since it had already been confiscated, quickly hatched a risky plan, his only hope. Before the soldiers reached the rear of the coach he collected the ID cards from the passengers and presented them politely and helpfully to the soldiers as they arrived, explaining that he had collected the documents to save them the effort and thanking them for their service.

The soldiers, mistaking him for a sympathiser, quickly scanned the documents and returned them for redistribution without making a thorough check. It was a terrifying experiment, but it worked and he crossed the border into safety. In due course he made his way to the Mediterranean Sea and thence, a month after his escape, into Israel.

Let me return to my oral examination, which concerned the question of whether I would admit to being Jewish under pain of death.

I searched my head for an answer. I knew that what they expected me to say would be too cheesy, but to admit that I wouldn't "put up my hand" would go against all I was trying to achieve. In fact, I replied quite honestly that I would not be brave enough to be the first to reveal my faith but I would not be the last (though how I would know whether or not I was going to be the last was a question I had not considered!).

The elders seemed pleased with my answer. They shook my hand and hugged me.

In reality, and in all honesty, I do not know how I would deal with such a situation should it arise.

I will have to wait and see.

4. Rebirth

Remarrying my wife – at 60
The elders questioned me about my marriage because Judaism accepts marriage only between two Jews. Although I was a convert, we could not be regarded as married from a Jewish perspective unless my wife also converted. It was even regarded as inappropriate for us to live together under our current circumstances. Consequently, on being questioned about whether my wife would consider joining the faith, I agreed we would discuss the matter.

It was yet another difficult question. Even though we were already married, I could not force conversion on my wife. If she would not convert it would put us in the awkward situation of being an unmarried couple in Jewish society. Although I had gone so far with my conversion, here I was at a crossroads once again, totally dependent on my wife's commitment. Blessedly, she had already started studying Judaism at the time of my conversion.

My wife, now a dedicated mother, a music graduate, a singing teacher and a recitalist, was at that time studying singing in New York. She accepted my determination to be Jewish and agreed to add the study of Judaism to her workload. I felt a deep appreciation for her cooperation.

Her efforts took six months with tuition from a Jewish scholar in New York and Rabbi Noach back in Tokyo. Her tuition, every two or three days, was less detailed though more frequent than mine.

Around that time my wife's music studies under the Jewish vocalist Emmy Burton had a philosophical impact. She asked Emmy if 50 was too late to make a fresh start in singing, to which the latter replied that age was irrelevant. In fact, one of her students was well into her eighties.

Jews think nothing of age except in the case of certain ceremonies. They feel age is meaningless in the sight of G-d. The emphasis is on everyone being on an equal footing. The idea delighted my wife, who happily embraced our wedding in her 61st year.

My wife was interested in the relationship between classical singing and Jewish culture because many western operas and songs were derived from the Hebrew Bible and Jewish history. Giuseppe Verdi, the 19th century Italian composer, socialised in Jewish society. His opera "Nabucco" was based on the overthrow of the Jews by the Babylonians in what is now Iraq, and the much loved "Va, pensiero, sull'ali dorate" recollects the story of Jewish exile after the loss of the First Temple in Jerusalem. This is not only a song that Jews love to sing but is often referred to as the second national anthem of Italy.

Greek and Christian church music has been influenced by the choruses and prayer songs sung in the synagogues of Judea from ancient times. Nowadays, Jewish musicians and music producers are a major influence in the world of music.

My wife began to feel that the logical, universal taste for Jewish music helped the beauty of western music blossom.

My children did not seem surprised by my determination to convert. Perhaps they had noticed me studying the religion or had been told I was considering taking the step.

My wife and I remarried in winter 2007. My Jewish friends came despite the inconvenience of the celebration being held on a weekday morning. My children were there too, mildly complaining because we had timed it when they were busy. However, everyone was pleased for us – and for us this was our third wedding, which thrilled my wife enormously. We had had informal and formal weddings before in the traditional Japanese Shinto style, both in my wife's hometown of Tokyo and in Kyoto, where I was from. This time, forty years later, my wife shopped delightedly for her ring and a bouquet for our Jewish wedding.

Breaking the Wine Glass: Remembering Adversity in the Midst of Joy

Our Jewish wedding was required to conform to custom in five ways:

Challenges On the Road to Conversion

1. It had to be witnessed by a rabbi.
2. A certificate of marriage, the Ketubah, was required.
3. It had to be held under a four-poster tent, the Chuppah.
4. The groom was to present a ring to the bride.
5. A glass had to be broken by the groom.

Wedding venues can be anywhere, and either indoors or outside. Ours was in a tent set up inside a synagogue in Tokyo. Jewish weddings are much simpler than their Shinto or Christian equivalents, and in urgent cases can be held under a cloth hung on top of four poles. Casual dress is quite acceptable.

The letter of marriage contains the marriage agreement between the groom and the bride. Ours, written in English, pledges my responsibilities to my wife: to accord her high regard, to sustain her financially and physically and to promise her substantial payment in case of divorce. The contents of the letter are much the same as in ancient times. In those days, Jewish law dictated that divorces were only filed by husbands and served through religious courts where the judges were rabbis. Men were in a position of marked superiority so divorce rules were designed to give women some protection.

Our wedding ceremony was simple. My bride wore a veil to cover her face till the end of the procedure. It was a reminder of the traditional Japanese headwear, or *tsunokakushi*, which veils the bride's horns of jealousy, ego and selfishness. It was also meant to symbolise the bride's resolve to become a gentle and obedient wife.

The rabbi said a prayer of blessing in front of us. Next, my wife and I shared a glass of wine before I crushed the glass under my foot. Then all three of us signed the letter of marriage commitment, which the rabbi read out loud.

Converting to Judaism

I placed the ring on my wife's hand and kissed her. The marriage was complete and the ceremony ended.

As was customary, the wedding ring was simple and, as advised by the rabbi, inexpensive.

The significance of the glass crushing was also explained to us. It was to remind us of the destruction of the Holy Temple in Jerusalem by the Roman commander Titus Flavius Vespasianus in AD 70. The Temple had been the centre of Judaism and the focal point of the Jewish religion. The famous 'Wailing Wall' in Jerusalem is a remnant of the temple and, though now a world-renowned tourist destination, it is still first and foremost the Noble Sanctuary for all Jews. Breaking a bottle of champagne at the launch of a ship has the same origin as our gesture. The glass crushing also reminds us of the fragility of marriage and is a statement of recognition of the frictions and rifts that can lie along the road of married life. In comparison, the Japanese marriage ceremony avoids confronting any of the realities of married life

This was my third wedding to my wife. It left us feeling refreshed, rejuvenated and grateful for our wonderful relationship. We had every incentive to make this marriage a continuation of the relationship that had gone before.

In due course, in 2009 my daughter also chose to marry her fiancé, a fellow student at Harvard Business School, through the inexpensive, no-fuss Jewish system. Though neither of them was Jewish, this system had the flexibility to accommodate their wedding.

Public Catechism and Jewish Renaming

Now, back to my examination. I had one final test after the interview. First of all I sang in Hebrew the prayer song "Shema Yisrael", known by all Jews, in front of a Jewish synagogue congregation. This was followed by a question-and-answer session with the rabbi, also in Hebrew.

I needed to memorise the song, questions and answers by listening to recordings since I was not yet fluent in Hebrew. The questions and answers concerned my oath to be a Jew, to believe in G-d and to abide by Jewish obligations.

Regarding the song "Shema Yisrael", which means "Hear o Israel", it is a pledge of one's faith in G-d and encapsulates the monotheistic essence of Judaism by emphasising: "The Lord is our G-d, the Lord is One. You shall love the Lord your G-d with all your heart and with all your soul and with all your might."

My ceremony was held in spring 2007, in a synagogue attended by tens of Jewish Tokyo residents. I expressed my commitment to be a Jew in Hebrew and was hugged and received a blessing as confirmation of my reception by the Jewish community.

To complete my conversion I took the Jewish name Yitzhak, to be written on my certificate of conversion. I chose it from a list of established Biblical Jewish names – many of which are the origins of Christian names. It is rendered as Isaac in Western Europe. My wife chose Ribhqeh, more generally known as Rebecca in the West.

In the strict Hebrew tradition, Jews did not have family names until modern times. Instead they were referred to as 'son of'. So, my name became Yizhak ben Abraham where 'ben' is Hebrew for 'son'. Needless to say, I am still perfectly comfortable with 'Kanji Ishizumi', my long-established name, but am slowly becoming accustomed to my Jewish title and feel like a new person whenever Yitzhak ben Abraham is used.

The Mikvah: Rebirth as a Jew

The very last ceremony was Mikvah, an immersion in water. It symbolises a convert's rebirth as a Jew. As such it is an unnecessary ceremony for anyone born into Judaism.

The word 'baptism' originates from the Greek translation of the Hebrew word Mikvah. So I daresay the Christian equivalent of Mikvah is baptism, though I have heard that at most Christian communions water is only applied to the forehead of the person being baptised.

Mikvah requires total immersion under natural water such as rainwater or seawater, and as such it must not pass through a man-made conduit such as a pump or pipe. The naked convert immerses his freshly washed body completely while a rabbi prays. The symbolism is most likely of a new-born child leaving the mother's amniotic fluid. It represents the rebirth of a convert to Judaism.

In the past, Mikvah was practised for cleansing the body before religious rituals until the time of the destruction of the Holy Temple in Jerusalem by the Roman army. It remained as a ritual before having sex on the seventh day after a woman's menstrual period. Today, however, few Jews practice the custom so fervently, though instead they wash their hands before prayer.

In the case of women, a male rabbi prays, facing away for modesty, while in the sea or on the beach.

My wife had her Mikvah one winter's day on a Tokyo shore accompanied by Rabbi Noach, with a helper and me standing watching from further up the shore. She walked into the water from the beach to submerge herself twice, completely, and afterwards declared she had felt "chilled to the bone".

Challenges On the Road to Conversion

My Mikvah also took place in Tokyo, in a synagogue with Rabbi Noach, in 2007. I will never forget his confirming words: "Now you have been reborn as a Jew."

None of us is aware of our actual birth. However, regarding my rebirth I had been aware of every step of the procedure and had even chosen the timing myself.

Jewish ceremonies may have little meaning to those outside our faith. However, for me they gave me a new education as well as allowing me to confirm my commitment. I also know I will feel ever grateful to the Rabbi and my fellow Jews who did so much to help me along the road.

There have been times when I have lost confidence and have sometimes been confused along the way. However, now I feel that everything was leading to this conversion and the outcome gives me a profound sense of destiny.

Not so many of us experience rebirth and the acquisition of new brethren. Looking back on my wonderful life, I have many people to thank. I look forward to the addition of a new 'family' and to my new Jewish life being wonderful, too.

CHAPTER 4

Jewish Life –
A Simple Life Brings Happiness

1. The Value of Rituals

Rituals and their Meanings: Being a Practising Jew
An octogenarian friend from Kyoto questioned me about Judaism. She was a Shingon Buddhist and a fervent believer of both Fudo Buddha and the Goddess of Good Fortune, the typical fusion of Shinto with Buddhism. She posed some of the most common questions about Judaism, as follows:

She: To whom do Jews genuflect? Jesus Christ?
I: Christians worship Christ. Jews don't.
She: Then what or who do Jews worship?
I: We don't worship anything.
She: Don't you have anything tangible to represent your G-d, like the shape of a Buddha?
I: No, but we read our Holy Book and study it at Saturday Service.

Jewish Life – A Simple Life Brings Happiness

She: Wow, that's so strange. Is that all you do?
I: No. We have rules and customs. For example, certain foods are forbidden to us and on one day each week we neither work nor study.
She: It all sounds rather quaint to me but certainly not like a religion.

So the conversation with the lady went.
The life of the Jew revolves around the following:

1. Maintaining a study of our Bible.
2. Adhering to our *kosher* diet, that is to say eating according to Jewish law.
3. Maintaining the rules of the Sabbath.
4. Adopting the 613 Jewish Commandments.

We are most seriously obligated to adhere to the first three of these requirements, though the 613 Commandments also play an important part in Jewish life.

To further expand on Jewish life:

Worship is not a rite since we do not worship anything tangible. Instead, we have discussions and studies. Sermons given at the synagogue by rabbis are lessons on Judaism, on which we base discussions.

We must pray three times every day – morning, noon and night – and on Saturday morning we attend the synagogue for morning devotion. During morning devotion we wear talliths and tefillin and in the Synagogue we always wear a hat called a kipa.

Tefillin are small black boxes that we wear, one on the head and the other on the upper inner left arm above the bicep. They are attached to us in a very specific way with leather thongs. The boxes contain parchment on which is written words from the Torah. According to Jewish tradition, the right hand represents love and the left justice, so the teffilah is attached to the left arm to deter us from brandishing justice in a dogmatic way.

The tallith is a prayer shawl with tassels and knots and blue or black stripes. The knots represent commandments to which the wearer should adhere. When wearing it we need to say a specific prayer in Hebrew. We wear the tallith only in the mornings and for Saturday prayers. It is specifically to remind us of our reason for being a Jew.

The kipa could be a hat in any style, though these days large ones hardly suit our modern lifestyle. Consequently, most men wear a small round covering on the top of their heads. It is to remind us of the Creator who placed us in the world.

We attach a parchment of Hebrew verses on the right side of the door or doorpost of our houses or offices, usually enclosed in a box of about 20 cm in length. This is called a Mezuzah. Mezuzah cases are produced from a wide variety of materials including metals, ceramics and even polymers.

In addition, our dietary restrictions, too numerous to list here, cover foodstuffs as well as methods of preparation. Strictest adherence would mean the simplest diet of vegetables, fruit and nuts.

We cannot work or play at all from Friday night to Saturday sunset so that we can nourish our minds, relaxing and releasing them from stresses and extraneous distractions.

We participate in regular festivals which, unlike our Japanese ones, are not always fun. For example, during

Jewish Life – A Simple Life Brings Happiness

Yom Kippur, the Day of Atonement, between September and October, we fast throughout a 25-hour period. During Sukkot, in autumn, we make a booth under the sky and stay in it for seven nights. Festivals strengthen cooperation and solidarity with fellow members of our local community.

Modern lifestyles are not exactly compatible with our various restrictions, though we must try our best. For instance my business, which takes me to New York, Los Angeles, Beijing, Shanghai, Hong Kong or Singapore, can make adherence to our practices rather tricky.

The Mezuzah: A Spiritual Reminder

In general, Japanese people would find Jewish life strange since Jews are perceived to live at the opposite extreme to the recognised Japanese lifestyle.

Jews give themselves little enjoyment of life, always studying and not eating anything tasty. Though Judaism does not demand that we forgo our desires for food and sex, it does require that we satisfy these natural urges in accordance with Jewish rules and, in a sense, our lives are certainly restricted by such rules. I should therefore add here that the rules we adhere to, as specified in the Bible by G-d, are the rules of restraint and self-discipline, which give a harmonious structure to life within our society. Although many ordinary Japanese people might regard our lifestyle as rather strange, those of us who practise it find it both very normal and most agreeable.

I am becoming accustomed to Jewish rituals and find that the repetition of them changes me subtly. For example, like all Jews, I now touch the Mezuzah on the door quite naturally each time I enter and leave a room. It is now second nature for me to wear the kipa and tallith, and I am completely comfortable with daily prayers and dietary restrictions. I comply with these requirements without ever asking myself why I do so.

We have many religious ceremonies, the repetition of which seems to offer a sense of belonging and reassurance. Perhaps this is why, according to an American report, religiously active people tend to live longer and more healthily than others. Many individuals play active roles in the synagogue beyond their eighties and are readily allocated jobs to perform.

Let us recall the traditional Jewish story of "the fish out of water" whereby the fish took the water totally for granted, pre-occupied only by thoughts of food, until G-d removed it for a brief moment – at which point it thought it would die.

In this regard, many of us are preoccupied by the pursuit of business, money, success or gourmet food but forget the importance of matters of religious and ethical thought, which keep the mind healthy. In his book *The Little Prince* Saint-Exupéry explained that "what is really important in life is unseeable". We are surrounded by vital things that possess neither colour nor flavour, neither sunlight nor moonlight, neither shape nor form. Perhaps rituals open our eyes to them.

Although I may not be reproached for neglecting our rituals and disciplines, nor for that matter will I be guaranteed to go to Heaven just by being a Jew. The repetition of rituals has made me feel the need to adhere to our disciplines. Their observance places me at ease. Though I used to regard ritual as irrational nonsense I now appreciate it and find myself surprised by my inner transition.

2. The Significance of Jewish Family Life

The Emotional and Physical Benefits of a Day of Rest
The hectic life I commenced on entering university intensified once I became internationally active as a lawyer, constantly moving between different time zones. I worked around the clock, stating that work was both my life and hobby.

Practising the custom of Sabbath has improved my physical and psychological health. Jews must not perform any work on the Sabbath and, though this meant I would lose 15% of my income, I decided to observe the rule.

I had previously had the following conversation with Rabbi Noach when learning about the Sabbath:

I: I am wondering if it will be acceptable to open my law firm for my staff to work on the Sabbath.
Rabbi: Our mindset is flexible on this. As long as you make the contracts on other days, any of your non-Jewish staff can carry out the work on Sabbath.
I: What is the Jewish opinion regarding interest generated on the Sabbath?
Rabbi: In Judaism no interest is generated from money borrowed from or lent between Jews nor between a Jew and a gentile residing in a Jewish country. However, it is acceptable if interest is generated on the money of gentiles in foreign lands.
I: This is tough.
Rabbi: Well, this is how Jewish business evolved: Regarding employment, in the old days feudal lords made villagers work without contracts. As for money-lending, such businesses could not

grow because they were regarded as sinful among Christians. Jews reaped the benefit by both employing gentiles, even on the Sabbath, on contract and also by being the only ones to embrace money-lending as a business.

As a consequence of our conversations I began to experience, for the first time, a period set aside for nothing other than religious activities. It made me feel really great. All activity connected with work or study which engages the brain causes stress. In my previous life I just worked on and on, always telling myself that I was feeling OK even though it was mentally and physically wearing. By the time I hit my fifties I was making myself quite ill. I now realise this would not have happened had I converted before then.

I now think of G-d, or life, or something abstract when I disconnect from work. My health has improved and my view widened. I even find that my brain works better after Sabbath.

My Sabbath experience has had a more general influence for the good in allowing me to discover the value of being disconnected from non-vital information such as politicians' remarks, stock prices or murders. I used to read voluminous work-related documents while also making time to read newspapers and magazines as well as watching the TV news in order to keep up with the times. Now, though I must assimilate huge amounts of information relevant to my work every day, I focus only on what I need. Now I do not read newspapers even on weekdays and I avoid the radio, TV and the temptation to click for internet news. I feel vastly better for it.

Jewish Life – A Simple Life Brings Happiness

Thousands of years ago Jews must have discovered the benefit of cutting themselves off from superfluous information just for one day each week. My readers, I recommend you try it: just spend one day in seven in peace and tranquillity with your family. If you do, I am sure you will be able to see the world differently.

Non-Kosher Foods: Religiously Proscribed
Our health is obviously affected by what we eat. Judaism is profoundly concerned with this matter, having detailed rules on diet called *kashrut*. Meals cooked in accordance with *kashrut* are called *kosher*. *Kosher* restaurants are now in fashion in the US for healthy dieters. *Kosher* food is highly regarded as absolutely safe and healthy in Europe and the US, so food marked as *kosher* has become very popular among the masses.

Kosher food is regarded as healthy and accords with today's stringent dietary principles. It is based around a low-calorie fruit and vegetable regime which shuns fatty delights.

Jews are agriculturalists rather than hunters. In fact, we are against eating wild animals, most likely to avoid the possible ingestion of animal-borne disease.

The Hebrew Bible says "The lion will eat straw." (Isaiah: C11 V7). This is even more relevant to humans. The Book of Genesis explains that G-d had prohibited man from eating meat. After the Great Flood He allowed it but only on condition that it contained neither blood nor fat. The effect was to make meat-eating rather difficult to practise.

The complicated processes required to remove blood and fat from meat discourage busy people from eating it because of the inconvenience involved.

When Jews do eat meat, the animal must be bled the moment it is killed. Any blood remaining in the meat must next be removed through immersion in salt water and only then can it be cooked, either by stewing or roasting. We are not allowed to eat raw meat.

We consider the consumption of blood and animal fat unhealthy and a cause of illness and obesity.

In Genesis in the Hebrew Bible, the following warning is made regarding breaching the rules for eating meat:

"If the rules are broken the earth's vegetation will cease to grow, fruit will no longer develop in the trees, paths will turn to desert, epidemics will become widespread and towns will crumble into ruin."

This is interesting in view of today's global environmental issues. Livestock consumes vast quantities of grain which, via their digestive systems, produces environmentally damaging methane gas at an alarming rate. Furthermore, livestock requires grazing land as well as that for the production of animal feed, and this in turn encourages global deforestation, increasing the prevalence of greenhouse gas, including carbon dioxide. Over time this has contributed to what we now recognise as serious global warming, which has caused extremes in weather and the expansion of deserts. G-d undoubtedly predicted this outcome.

We are allowed to eat chicken, duck and turkey as well as herbivorous livestock such as cows, sheep and goats, but pork is strictly taboo. It would seem that pigs are particularly susceptible to developing and transmitting infections and were most likely responsible for the flu epidemic of 2009. We are therefore healthier if we exclude them from our diet.

Jewish Life – A Simple Life Brings Happiness

Dairy foods must conform to strict production specifications, and the cooking of food which combines milk and meat is prohibited since it is considered that milk is purely for the development of the young of the animals that produce it. From a medical standpoint this tends to limit our intake of high-fat foods.

We have detailed the proscription regarding the consumption of seafood, though it forms an important part of Jewish diet. In accordance with the Misnah we can eat fish with fins and round, easily-removable scales, such as herring, sardines and salmon, among saltwater fish, and trout and carp among freshwater fish. Japanese Jews cannot indulge in their favourite food of sushi!

We regard eel, rockfish and puffer fish as inedible, since they do not have scales – or their scales are not removable – and fish categorised as benthic feeders, which live on the seabed, are forbidden. This means halibut, sole, prawns, squid, langoustine, eel, shellfish, sea urchin, oysters, clams and molluscs are out of bounds.

Also forbidden are deepwater scaleless fish such as tuna, swordfish, whale, dolphin and bonitos, and we must avoid that delicacy caviar. However, one positive result is that we are less prone than many to food poisoning and the effects of sea pollution.

With my pre-conversion fish diet on a Japanese scale, a US health check revealed my heavy metal contamination to be ten times greater than the American average. Since cutting most seafood from my diet 10 years ago, this has now come down to the US norm. Consequently, I feel that the Jewish ruling on seafood conforms neatly to modern-day medical thinking.

Eating to Live versus Living to Eat

Though we do have dietary restrictions, there are certain foodstuffs that are highly recommended by the Bible and regarded as G-d's blessings.

They include grapes, wheat, barley, figs, olives, pomegranates and honey.

Wine made from grapes is regarded as a Holy drink and a symbol of joy. We are supposed to pray as a kind of ritual before drinking wine, and even babies are given a small sip in order to become used to it at a tender age. However, drunkenness is unacceptable because it hinders us from pursuing our obligation to pray coherently, three times each day.

Ritual fasting, eleven times per year for the devout, is another aspect of our culture. This is wonderful for giving the digestive system a break and clearing out the intestines. It also allows digestive enzymes to recover and activates an important macrobiotic gene. A Jew who strictly observes the dietary code will eat mostly grains, fruit and vegetables. We rarely dine out because very few restaurants observe *kashrut*.

After attending a lecture at Harvard University's Stem Cell Institute I noted that their findings regarding eating less plus the benefits of a fruit and vegetable diet conform to Jewish thinking.

In Japan we say "Moderate eating keeps the doctor away." Harvard researchers recommend a daily intake of around 1100 kcal/day, which is exactly half of the Japanese average consumption. Although the Japanese enjoy the longest lifespan as things stand, it could be argued that they would have a healthier life in old age if they ate less. It is quite possible that fewer would become bedridden or disabled.

Jewish Life – A Simple Life Brings Happiness

A Jewish diet could form a good balanced basis on which to reduce the average family intake. Jewish doctors I have met enthuse about the health benefits of a *kosher* diet and its medical soundness. Indeed, Jewish concepts regarding health and food are regarded as scientifically sound even by modern-day standards yet, amazingly, they have been in place for hundreds of years.

3. Judaism: the Significance of Humour

Overcoming Life's Trials with Laughter
My comments on strict Jewish rules may create the impression that Jews are very formal people. However, I discovered that their lives are full of cheerful laughter.

Rabbi Noach tried a Jewish joke on me some two years after commencing his teaching. When I didn't find it at all funny he said that I had a long road to travel.

The joke, a story of a bakery in a freezing Moscow under the Stalin regime, is as follows:

People arrived at the shop at 5am to form a long queue for the freshly baked bread.

The baker arrived to open the shop at 7am shouting at the queue that he had no bread to sell to Jews today, though he had not yet started baking.

The Jews in the queue walked away.

At 9 o'clock the baker announced that he would have no bread to sell to the citizens of Moscow, so they too left.

By 10 o'clock the only ones remaining were Soviet military officers, who were expecting their usual extra ration.

At 11 o'clock the baker announced that due to a non-delivery of flour there would be no bread at all, even for officers.

So they angrily shouted, "See! Once more the Jews get the best deal!"

It was obvious to the rabbi that I did not understand the joke so he filled me in on some background knowledge:

Jews have never been given preferential treatment anywhere and those living under the Stalin regime were particularly discriminated against. Jews rarely received bread apart from on the rare occasions when there was a surplus to sell.

The joke was that since Jews were not going to receive any bread they had not had to suffer the inconvenience of waiting for hours in the freezing cold and had had the luxury of going home. This made the officers extremely angry and once more they resentfully blamed their misfortunes on the Jews.

Rabbi Noach tried to teach me how Jews made humour of their plight as a way of coping with it. He didn't really expect me to understand such humour since I had no experience of constant and persistent discrimination. He felt it important that, as a convert, I should understand how Jews often overcome adversity through ironic humour and laughter.

Jewish Wit and Wisdom

Interestingly, the Hebrew word *chockman* means both 'joke' and 'wisdom'. So Jews have probably understood the huge benefits of laughter from way back in their history.

Humour tends to blossom under oppression. The people of the Soviet Union and Eastern Europe were famous for it and aggrieved Jews were no exception. Their jokes helped them survive extraordinary pressures.

Laughter can be a profound activity used to ridicule the oppressor as well as uniting people against him or her.

Jewish Life – A Simple Life Brings Happiness

It is impossible to censor because it is a natural bodily function.

Jewish humour requires knowledge, wit, wisdom and perception plus the sense of humour to understand the joke. Sometimes it requires one to have a quick and sophisticated intellect.

My study of Jews made me realise that much about their humour and cheerfulness had developed through their suffering.

CHAPTER 5

How Doubt Gives Rise to Knowledge

1. Nothing in this World is Certain

Shades of Grey vs Black and White
Observing situations carefully, we find they often possess multiple facets. That is to say, we can see them and analyse them in a multitude of often opposing ways.

Let me examine as an example the story of Noah's Ark in chapter 6 of Genesis in the Hebrew Bible:
Suffering sadness for the rampant evil that had descended on earth, G-d attempted to wash it away in the Great Flood though He saved the innocent Noah and his family. Noah took a male and female of every creature into the ark to save them from the flood. However, right and wrong, bad and good, toxic and pure, blessing and misfortune, poverty and wealth were admitted too.

Since then, all events have opposite consequences so, for instance, someone's loss will tend to be someone else's gain.

How Doubt Gives Rise to Knowledge

I asked the rabbi why Almighty G-d allowed Hitler to exist. Hitler and his Nazis, who committed the ultimate crime of the Holocaust, were, after all, G-d's creation.

The rabbi explained that, on the one hand we are not fully able to understand G-d's will and, on the other, he gave every man free will, and that since men possess both good and evil characteristics there will always be good and evil, right and wrong in our society.

In my legal work I have encountered many hypocrites who portray an image of sweet innocence on the surface yet underneath are quite unsavoury characters. Conversely, I found that some portrayed as evil turned out to be good people. In light of these experiences the Jewish view on the coexistence of good and bad makes sense.

This turns out to be the case at a national level with international standards. The USA tends to enforce "what is right" in countries all over the world. US norms regarding money laundering regulation, bank and securities regulation, the Securities Exchange Act and accounting practices have all become global standards. As far as I can ascertain, American politicians and businessmen genuinely believe that the rest of the world must use what the US defines as correct and logical systems.

At the same time, the Americans pursue their own advantage by creating the systems, complete with discreet corporate tax avoidance ruses hidden within for themselves and their wealthy clients.

We need to be philosophical about each individual case when viewing the world from the perspective of two sides. We should be aware of both sides of a "good" person because good and evil so often go together. We should benefit from the Jewish perspective on this.

2. Readiness to Accept Others

Netsuke Collection: Shrewd Investment and Risk Management
Though I am not a collector, I have been studying *netsuke* in connection with my family's art-fan business.

A *netsuke* is a delicately-made, carved functional ornament which Japanese people hung on their purses, pipe cases, cigarette boxes or pill boxes by means of a fine silk cord during the Samurai period. They are like lucky charms. In those days Japanese people did not use pockets, so the boxes with attached *netsuke* hung decoratively from their waist bands on silk twine.

Netsuke are highly appreciated and marketable miniature ornaments. They often appear in oriental artwork auctions at well-known sale rooms such as Christie's, Sotheby's or Bonhams. There is an International Netsuke Society originating in the USA with its own Japanese art researchers whose interest also encompasses *ojime*, a *netsuke*-like carved bead used as a button in conjunction with the *netsuke*. Many Society members, and collectors of both, are Jewish.

My best friend, optometrist Dr Joe Kirstein, was the chairman of the Society. He has been a close family friend for many years and, as a Russian Jew, was thrilled to learn about my own conversion. He informed me about *netsuke* and the Jewish connection

Jews interested in *netsuke* are often motivated to learn Japanese and almost all of the speakers at the

How Doubt Gives Rise to Knowledge

Society conferences can read and speak our language. I often wonder if there is a similarity between Jewish and Japanese aesthetics. Certainly Jews are interested in learning about and studying foreign artworks and in particular those from Japan.

However, one obvious reason why Jews are particularly interested in *netsuke* and *ojime* is that they are small, very portable and very easily converted into cash, like diamonds and jewellery. After the large-scale and widespread robberies connected with the Holocaust and other atrocities, it has become almost engrained among Jewish people to take an interest in easily portable, valuable, saleable investment items.

True *netsuke* masterpieces can sell to wealthy collectors around the world for tens of millions of yen (£1 = 182 yen at the time of writing) and, unlike other artworks, they are not affected by trends and fashion. They are easily stored and transported compared to fragile pottery and huge paintings and, probably because of this ease of risk manageability, their values are invariably high. As investment items they conform perfectly to Jewish requirements.

The Joy of Discussion – "Gold under the Tip of your Tongue"

"Gold under the tip of your tongue" and "happiness from the tip of your tongue" are Jewish sayings which imply that happiness can be achieved by promoting better understanding through discussion and questioning. At the same time they mean that making someone happy with compliments will bring oneself happiness.

A society's proverbs convey its nature. Japanese proverbs referring to the tongue, such as "lines from the tip of your tongue" and "forked tongue", are rather negative. In Japan, discussion and debate are regarded with contempt whereas silence is a major virtue.

Jews feel integrated when they receive questions and counterargument. They value dialogue. Conversely, discussions lead to blows between the Japanese, who regard counterargument as personal criticism. The Japanese need to negotiate extremely carefully and diplomatically behind the scenes.

Another Jewish proverb, "Say a thousand, know a hundred", means a great deal of knowledge can be gained by questioning constantly. The Japanese saying "Say one, know ten" would not make sense in Jewish culture. The Japanese would appear to be receptive to only a fraction of the knowledge that the Jews find they can glean through discussion.

Jews thrive on voicing and comparing opinions, and love to initiate discussion even if through controversy. On the other hand, the Japanese communicate with flattery and ambiguity to skirt around controversial issues. I found the open manner of the Jews refreshingly pleasant.

Every culture and each ethnic group from the 190 countries in the world should be free to both have and voice their own opinions. If we do not speak out we cannot attract attention to ourselves and our needs. In this regard, Jews are particularly assertive.

One of the greatest Jewish thinkers, Hillel the Elder, said "A shy person cannot learn. Therefore he cannot understand G-d's will." This implies that a person who cannot question an issue cannot gain a proper understanding of it. The act of trying to understand differences in points

How Doubt Gives Rise to Knowledge

of view opens our eyes to different ways of thinking and interpreting. Jews use their voices to question various views, and consequently they broaden their minds.

CHAPTER 6

Making it Work as a Japanese Jewish Lawyer

1. Personal Evolution through Life-long Learning

Intellectual Curiosity and a Thirst for Knowledge
How did you find my experiences of the Jewish community and the process of conversion?
　In this chapter, I am going to see what we can learn from Jews.
　I had hungered for the meaning of life with a desire to have a faith like others in the world. Then, finding Judaism, I sought to study it. Judaism offered me the answers which satisfied the hunger in my heart. I now belong to a people and a religion and have gained the faith in monotheism and the Hebrew Bible that form a common bond among many of us in the world. My desires have been fulfilled.
　In addition, my mind has been quietly and continually changed by constant religious activity and I find it natural

to live my life according to Jewish principles while discovering a sense of peace. However, like other Jews, I still question the presence of G-d.

Though I will probably never fully understand G-d I will continually think of Him for the rest of my life. My mind has been changed through questioning and studying, and with regard to the presence of G-d these processes will also continue.

The intellectual reservoir of Judaism is bottomless and exciting, something I shall never tire of studying. Judaism fits me well as it requires neither fanaticism nor frenzied passion.

Through my inquisitiveness and the joy of studying I am constantly learning new things in relation to G-d.

Only through studying Judaism have I realised that intellectual growth continues constantly regardless of age.

An Intellectual Search for Truth

The principles of Judaism correspond to my experiences at work resolving legal disputes for my clients. However, the very complication which characterises human society means that very few disputes are straightforward.

If, in my field of business law, we pursue only what is right, we may not be able to represent some of our clients fully, while case times will inevitably be extended. However, I do try to consider the best interests of my clients, whatever their position in a dispute, unless it is absolutely contrary to social justice.

I think many people try to find the medium between the ideal and reality. I decided to question myself in respect of the meanings behind everything I was doing regardless of this consideration.

Then I encountered Judaism. Jews constantly try to understand G-d's will. Although they may never find the answers for which they might be searching, their priority is to continuously think about what G-d would regard as right. Their attitude is very similar to the one I developed through my work.

Searching for the truth is a humbling experience because it demonstrates to us our limitations in applying our wisdom. I believe that pursuing the truth develops our intellect even though the pursuit might be fruitless. It might even be argued that the evolution of our intellect resulted from the efforts of the inquisitive. Our advancement as a race and our appetite for study are closely connected.

Remember Rabbi Noach's counterargument about the evolution theory: "Would a human evolve from a kettle if it is left for 15 billion years?" Nobody nurtured in an educational system based on cramming could entertain such a huge idea. Only a brain honed through questioning could produce it.

Through my study of Judaism I realised it should be expected that great scientific thinkers and inventors would emerge from the Jews, who had been trained to think and reason from early childhood. Furthermore, I have come to realise that inquisitiveness improves behaviour and increases our happiness.

"Learning during your tender years will steer you towards a great career in the prime of manhood. Learning in the prime of manhood will help ensure that your mind will remain young when you get old. Learning in old age will ensure you won't decay after you die." So said Issai Sato, a Japanese Confucian scholar of the Edo Period. Great thinkers from every era of civilisation have always shown a common understanding of the value of learning.

Maintaining an Open Mind

Jewish history influenced my thoughts. Jews have always shown an interest in anything they know little about, including different peoples and cultures. They seem to possess the most curious nature and also believe there is no certainty in life.

Although I always felt I conducted myself towards others in a tolerant manner, without realising it I had fit myself into a preconceived mould, basing my judgements on assumptions. The Jewish way of thinking flexibly showed me that I was trapped by preconceptions of which I now had to rid myself.

These days I view subjects from a multifaceted perspective, approaching life and health differently by thinking about the meaning of everything I do. This enables me to reflect on my work, interpersonal interactions and my inner self.

My reward is to have my interests broadened in respect of the spiritual world in which Jews live. The Jewish people, who most recently suffered the Nazi Holocaust, have come through a history of grief and suffering beyond all imagination from the perspective of my peaceful life.

The Polish Melamed family were fairly typical, escaping to Japan from Lithuania with their young son Leo, using transit passes issued by the sympathetic Japanese ambassador Chiune Sugihara, in order to save their lives.

Young Leo, who left Japan for the USA, went on to become chairman on the Chicago Mercantile Exchange, creating the International Money Market in the 1970s and becoming famous as the "Father of Financial Futures".

However, because of his early experiences, throughout his life he voiced the warning "Be cautious, the devil could be lying in wait around the next corner."

Ambassador Sugihara is remembered with gratitude for saving the lives of a further 6000 Jews.

The investor and philanthropist, George Soros, well known as "the Man Who Broke the Bank of England", ran away from his home in Nazi-occupied Hungary. He recalls, "The risks and gambles I took in dealing with currency and market fluctuations are insignificant compared to those my father and I faced together when I was a teenager."

Jews have always demonstrated a resilience to survive suffering and a moral strength based on their culture, history and inner inquisitiveness. I am thrilled to have been accepted as one of them thanks to the patience and help of Rabbi Noach.

2. Japan: a Country with Claims to Monoculturalism

The Japanese would do well to follow the lead of progressive Jewish culture yet they ignore the huge potential of the many foreigners living within the nation.

It is disheartening to see how Japan seems to have closed ranks even more tightly since the collapse of its bubble economy. It tightens regulations to discourage foreign investment and seems to take an unfavourable view towards businesses with overseas connections.

In 2006, the American investment company Steel Partners filed a suit against the Japanese Bulldog Sauce Company in the Tokyo District Court over its anti-takeover defence measures. As expected, the court ruled against Steel, terming it an "abusive acquirer" and a "vulture investor" without defining precisely what these terms meant. The court seemed oblivious to the worldwide controversy it was creating.

I personally received tens of enquiries from potential overseas investors in connection with the court decision. However, the illogicality of the Japanese approach to international business is infamous among such professional investors.

Japanese business law seems to have a different basis from that in the Western world, where the basic principle is to protect the legal pursuit of profit across nations. The implication of the Japanese court's ruling is, to be blunt, that it simply does not like foreign money.

A further Japanese controversy that caused an international scandal was the court's ruling against Yoshiaki Murakami, the former president of the Murakami Fund. The judge stated, "I am horrified by his attitude of profit supremacy by buying at a lower price and selling at a higher price." Yet is this not the basis of any business, whether it be the selling of groceries, fish or stocks and shares? This case also created an international flood of correspondence into my in-tray. I could not explain what was happening because it was beyond understanding.

EPILOGUE

The Future: a Path of Spiritual Development
I hope my personal perspective on the Jewish lifestyle has interested you. As well as the Jewish way of thinking and living, I have endeavoured to cover my own studies pre-conversion, the issues created by circumcision and my own inner transition.

Of the little information on Jews previously available in Japan, some is incorrect and some even prejudiced. Researchers and journalists generally present a second- or third-hand view which, though perhaps partially correct, does not explain the picture accurately, directly 'from the horse's mouth' as I have tried to do.

I hope I have demonstrated that in reality the Jewish lifestyle differs considerably from the commonly held Japanese concept: one of wealth and excentricity.

I will be happy if you now have a clearer image of Jewish people and no longer feel they are beyond comprehension. However, I know that my writing will have precipitated many personal questions.

One Japanese person with some knowledge of Judaism plus a great desire for gourmet food expressed sadness that Jews did not know the delights of steak, pork shabu-shabu, fried prawns or sushi. Another felt he lived free from

Epilogue

constraints and did not want to be bound by Jewish precepts.

I might have felt the same before my conversion but now I am a new and different person. In accordance with the teachings of Judaism I dedicate myself to seeking the purpose and meaning of life according to G-d's will. This search would be extremely difficult – if not impossible – without precepts.

Humans face many temptations which might easily rule us and distract us from seeking 'The Truth' if we did not have precepts. Yet the study of Judaism can offer us far more mental and spiritual sustenance than booking into a luxury restaurant for a sumptuous meal.

Many of the things we see around us arouse desires, lusts and covetousness, which create within us feelings of jealousy, envy, frustration, anger and even sadness. Judaism teaches us to detach our minds from things we can see. I have found that by following our precepts I am far less affected by such negative feelings and much less under the influence of external happenings.

This all takes me back to our very own 'Japanese Tea Ceremony'. Why does it have so many rules of behaviour? Why does it involve the application of so many complex manners? Are all these things needed just to drink tea? No, not really, but they prepare participants to remove themselves from the chaos and stresses of life once ensconced in the tea room.

The same can be said about Judaism. Following its precepts restores peace into our minds and spirits by removing us from the distractions which surround us.

Our Bible stresses the importance of invisible, immeasurable virtues such as justice, love, mercy and goodness, and our religion teaches us to examine and question them.

The Sabbath is the day when we break free from our material world. My spiritual world has been expanding ever since I set aside the Sabbath to make myself think about spiritual matters.

I am aware that the Jewish way is just one of many lifestyles and, though I have chosen to become a Jew, I am still grateful for what I have learned through being brought up in my mother country of Japan, the home of my ancestors. I love my country and always wish the best for it.

Once Japan was brimful of enterprising spirit and its people appreciated the spiritual dimension of life. However, today's Japan appears to be a fragile country in economic and social confusion. Because the influential people in Japan appear to feel this was caused by overseas influences, the inward-looking urge to reduce international exchange is growing. Japan is in danger of losing the opportunities and economic vigour which exchanges with overseas societies can create. Couple this with a loss of spirituality and society loses its ethical base for living while, at the same time, social problems rise to the surface.

In contrast, Jewish life is centred around ethical teaching based on the content of the Hebrew Bible and Jews manage to turn their uniqueness into a strength. Their ideals, which have made them so successful, are quite different from those currently being adopted in Japan. In cross-examining themselves to find the route to general improvement, Japanese people could do well to give some time to examining the Jewish way.

I hope you too, dear reader, might find cause to reflect on your own life and society because of reading this book.

Epilogue

It might provide a pathway into happiness as well as the start of a route that could take people, not least the Japanese, forward into a brighter future.

Kanji Ishizumi
Shanghai, October 2009

Lightning Source UK Ltd.
Milton Keynes UK
UKOW05f1529270617
304208UK00001B/52/P